LIBERALISM

Political and economic systems either allow exchange and resource allocation to take place through mutual agreement under a system of liberalism, or force them to take place under a system of cronyism in which some people have the power to direct the activities of others.

This book seeks to clarify the differences between liberalism and cronyism by scrutinizing the actual operation of various political and economic systems. Examples include historical systems such as fascism in Germany between the world wars and socialism in the former Soviet Union, as well as contemporary systems such as majoritarianism and industrial policy.

By examining how real governments have operated, this book demonstrates why—despite their diverse designs—in practice all political and economic systems are variants of either liberalism or cronyism.

LIBERALISM AND CRONYISM: TWO RIVAL POLITICAL AND ECONOMIC SYSTEMS

by Randall G. Holcombe and Andrea M. Castillo

MERCATUS CENTER
George Mason University

Arlington, Virginia

Mercatus Center
George Mason University
3351 Fairfax Drive, 4th Floor
Arlington, VA 22201-4433
T: (703) 993-4930
mercatus.org

First printing, April 2013

                Library of Congress Cataloging-in-Publication Data

Holcombe, Randall G.
  Liberalism and cronyism : two rival political and economic systems /
Randall G. Holcombe, DeVoe Moore Professor of Economics, Florida State
University, Andrea M. Castillo, Mercatus Center at George Mason
University Arlington, Virginia.
      pages cm
  Includes bibliographical references.
  ISBN 978-0-9892193-0-3 (pbk.) -- ISBN 978-0-9892193-1-0 (e-book)
  1. Liberalism. 2. Corruption. 3. Capitalism. 4. Ideology. 5.
Political science. I. Title.
  JC574.H637 2013
  320.51--dc23
                        2013012825

Printed in the United States of America

CONTENTS

There are two fundamentally opposed means whereby
man, requiring sustenance, is impelled to obtain
the necessary means for satisfying his desires.
These are work and robbery, one's own labor and the forcible
appropriation of the labor of others ... [I call] one's own
labor and the equivalent exchange of one's own labor for
the labor of others, the "economic means" for the satisfaction
of needs, while the unrequited appropriation of the labor of
others will be called the "political means."

—*Franz Oppenheimer,* The State
(translated by John M. Gitterman)

Thieves respect property; they merely wish the property to
become their property that they may more perfectly respect it.

—*G. K. Chesterton,* The Man Who Was Thursday

INTRODUCTION

P EOPLE OFTEN SEE political and economic systems as interrelated and complementary. In the mid-twentieth century, Friedrich Hayek and Milton Friedman questioned whether political freedom could survive without economic freedom.[1] Joseph Schumpeter was pessimistic about the future of capitalism not because of any weaknesses in the economic system, but because he believed that the people who benefited from it the most were unwilling to support it politically.[2] Decades later, after the collapse of the Berlin Wall in 1989 and the breakup of the Soviet Union in 1991 that ended the Cold War, political scientist Francis Fukuyama called the triumph of capitalism and democracy the end of history,[3] meaning that capitalism and democracy were the ultimate evolution of economic and political systems.

Political and economic systems are designed to operate within a structure of rules—rules that provide the appearance that leaders make political and economic decisions based on objective criteria rather than based on payoffs to cronies who are close to those with political and economic power. As political scientist Murray Edelman points out,[4] rules not only govern the operation of political and economic systems, they also have symbolic value. The more people believe that the system is based on objective and unbiased rules, the easier it is to get citizens to conform to those rules. If citizens do not buy into the system, it will be dysfunctional at best, and will lead to rebellion and overthrow at worst. Thus, elaborate rules and the justifications for them lie at the foundation of all political and economic systems.

Whenever these systems fail to operate on a basis of mutual agreement and exchange, some people will be forced to act to benefit others. This force can come in the form of taxes, which require people to give up resources they otherwise would not; government regulations, which force people to act in ways they otherwise would not; or, in more extreme cases, state confiscation of people's property through eminent domain or confiscation of their lives by drafting them into national service. Despite the different structure of rules in the various political and economic systems, when someone with power decides who gets the government job, who qualifies for payments from the government, or who has to pay to provide benefits to others, cronyism cannot help but be a factor in those decisions. Rules and objective criteria notwithstanding, there are always subjective elements behind such decisions—decisions like who among many qualified applicants will be admitted to a college program or which firm will get the government contract. Furthermore, while rules have the appearance of objectivity, a political process influenced by favored interest groups creates those rules, resulting in cronyism.

Political and economic systems create a set of rules for dealing with scarcity, which means that all people cannot have everything they want. The rules determine who is entitled to what. Those who make the rules and those who have the power to make decisions under them can game the system to favor their cronies. In a liberal system, as we use the term "liberal" in this book, people are entitled to what they produce, and others can acquire their production only through voluntary agreement. When political and economic systems work though coercion, it is not surprising that those who have the power to coerce others end up profiting from that power, whether the power goes to a majority in a democracy or to a small ruling coalition in a dictatorship. Regardless of the appearance of objectivity, discretion creeps into the decision-making process, and that discretion benefits those who are cronies of the people who make the decisions.

The alternatives in any political or economic system reduce to liberalism or cronyism. Liberalism is a political philosophy that rests on the protection of individual rights and voluntary agreement when dealing with others. Cronyism is a system in which people we call "cronies" receive benefits from personal connections that are not available to others who are outside that group. Political and economic systems are typically characterized as capitalist, socialist, communist, fascist, despotic, progressive, corporatist, majoritarian, and so on. Despite the nuances that differentiate these systems, all must have some mechanism for coordinating the activities of everyone in the group, whether that group is a family, a club, a tribe, or a nation. In all cases, either people engage each other through mutual agreement and exchange, or some people have the power to direct the activities of others. When some people have the power to coerce others to undertake actions that they would not voluntarily agree to, personal connections inevitably creep in to benefit those who are cronies of the people who hold power.

The analysis that follows lays out a framework for understanding liberalism and cronyism. We then discuss the actual operation of different political and economic systems. Some of these analyses are heavily based on historical examples, such as fascism in Germany between the world wars and socialism in the former Soviet Union. Others look at contemporary political and economic systems such as majoritarianism and industrial policy. Through examining the operation of actual political and economic systems, we show why, despite their various designs, all political and economic systems in practice are variants of liberalism or cronyism. Either exchange and resource allocation take place through mutual agreement under a system of liberalism, or they take place through a system of cronyism where some people have the power to direct the activities of others.[5]

CHAPTER 1:
LAYING A FOUNDATION

BEFORE SETTING UP an exposition of different political and economic systems, we must first lay a foundation that will support our analysis. In order to differentiate liberalism from cronyism, we need to define our terms, understand the historical development of the ideas that undergird these competing systems, and recognize how government representatives actually make decisions rather than how we would like them to make decisions. The next few sections will cover these three areas and provide us with the tools to analyze different political and economic systems.

LIBERALISM, CLASSICAL AND CONTEMPORARY

WE USE THE terms "liberal" and "liberalism" in this book differently from the way they are used in contemporary American political discourse. Liberalism is a political philosophy based on the protection of individual rights and the interaction of individuals through voluntary agreement. This meaning goes back hundreds of years, but in the twenty-first century United States, "liberalism" has come to mean something different in political discourse.

People often use "liberalism" to mean "progressivism," a political philosophy based on the idea that in addition to protecting individuals' rights, government should improve people's economic well-being. In contemporary America "liberalism" and "progressivism" are often used interchangeably, and those who identify as contemporary liberals often refer to themselves as progressives. The Orwellian confusion in terminology has sometimes caused people who consider themselves liberals in the old sense of the word to refer to themselves as "classical liberals" or "libertarians." Throughout this book, we use "liberalism" in its original sense, as the political philosophy that limits the government's role to the protection of individual rights. A liberal society is one in which property rights are clearly defined and protected by the government and in which interpersonal interaction occurs through mutual agreement and exchange.

This metamorphosis in terminology is not unique to liberalism. For example, throughout the early twentieth century the word "welfare" was used to describe how well off people were, but now it has come to mean "public charity." The term "public charity" seemed to have a demeaning connotation and its supporters wanted to reduce the stigma attached to it, so they began calling it "welfare."[1] Similarly, taxes are often described as "contributions." The government does not "tax" workers to support Social Security; workers make "contributions" to the program. Political discourse often modifies terminology so that government policies based on coercion, that take from some to give to others, sound less oppressive, less coercive, and more voluntary. We prefer to use "liberalism" in its original sense rather than consent to the hijacking of the term to describe a political philosophy that is antithetical to its original meaning.

LIBERALISM AND CRONYISM

JOHN LOCKE, AN early liberal thinker, used the concept of self-ownership as a foundation for developing his political philosophy.[2] People own themselves, Locke argued, and therefore own their labor. When people combine their labor with unowned resources, the product of their labor becomes their property. Locke established a moral foundation for the market economy based on the political foundation of individual rights. The idea of individual rights is generally accepted in the twenty-first century, but it was a revolutionary idea when Locke put it forward in the seventeenth century. The Founding Fathers often cited Locke's ideas as the intellectual foundation for the American and French Revolutions that followed toward the end of the eighteenth century.[3]

The revolutionary nature of Locke's liberal ideas becomes apparent when contrasted with the ideas of Thomas Hobbes, who wrote a few decades earlier that the only way to escape from a life of anarchy, where life would be "nasty, brutish, and short" and a war of all against all, was to establish a society where everyone obeyed the rules of the sovereign.[4] The sovereign was the political ruler, and could be a king, a dictator, or a democratically elected government. Hobbes argued that whatever the form or ruler, everyone had to obey the government to prevent chaos and anarchy. In Hobbes's view, the government granted rights and people were obligated to obey the government's rules. Locke, however, saw a world where people naturally had rights and the government's role was to protect those rights. If the government failed in this function, Locke believed that the people had the right to overthrow and replace their government.

Liberalism begins with the Lockean recognition that people have rights and the government's role is to protect those rights. The rights individuals have to themselves and to their property imply that individuals may interact with each other only through voluntary agreement. In the economic sphere, this idea means that people engage in economic activity through voluntary exchange, which gives rise to markets and market transactions. A liberal government limits itself to protecting individuals' rights to make such exchanges and does not interfere with transactions people want to undertake voluntarily.

Cronyism is a system in which people receive benefits from personal connections—benefits that are not available to individuals who are outside that group of cronies. The possibility of cronyism exists any time some people have the power to impose their will on others. If some people can use force to take resources from others, there will be a natural tendency for those in power to transfer resources to those who have political connections, family connections, or other personal connections to them.

There are only two possibilities for how the ownership of economic resources can be transferred. Resources can be transferred to someone else by the voluntary agreement of the resource owner, typically in a mutually beneficial exchange, or resources can be coercively taken from one person and given to another. This second method of transfer leads to cronyism. The truth of this bold claim is not apparent at first, because it is easy to argue that resources can be taken from some for the common good of all. For example, a government could establish a system of taxes and use the tax revenue to provide roads, police protection, and other public goods. However, just because a government could establish such a system does not mean a government actually will. Even if government provides roads that everyone can use, someone must determine which firm gets the construction contract to build the road, how much will be spent, and where the road will go. Special interests weigh in heavily on such decisions, and people with political connections tend to be favored in the outcomes. That is cronyism.

Some people might cite the United States as an example of a nation in which the government collects taxes to produce outputs that promote the public good, but others argue that crony capitalism is undermining the market economy and democratic government in the United States.[5] To sort out the competing claims, we must undertake an analysis of political and economic systems to see how they actually work.

Ludwig von Mises, analyzing political philosophy before it was subject to economic analysis, argued that political philosophers

> did not search for the laws of social cooperation because they thought that man could organize society as he pleased. If social conditions did not fulfill the wishes of the reformers, if their utopias proved unrealizable, the fault was seen in the moral failure of man. Social problems were considered ethical problems. What was needed in order to construct the ideal society,

they thought, was good princes and virtuous citizens.[6]

Mises was arguing that there are laws that govern political and economic interactions among individuals, and that political and economic systems can only be understood within the framework of those laws. A good place to begin analyzing the claim that all political and economic systems are variants of liberalism or cronyism is with an economic analysis of government decision-making.

THE MYTH OF THE OMNISCIENT, BENEVOLENT DICTATOR

POLICY ANALYSIS IN modern economics typically takes place by comparing some state of affairs in an economy (sometimes a real state of affairs, sometimes an imagined or assumed one) to an ideal allocation of resources. Economic analysis notes the differences between the current state of affairs and the ideal state of affairs, with the idea that the government, armed with this information, can correct the market's failure to allocate resources efficiently and attain this ideal state.[7] This approach has been used for more than half a century in economic analysis and remains current in the twenty-first century. The proof by economists Kenneth Arrow and Gerard Debreu of the uniqueness and stability of a competitive equilibrium also supports this line of reasoning.[8] Arrow and Debreu showed that there is one unique, stable, optimal allocation of resources in a competitive economy, and this allocation is the benchmark for economic efficiency. An economy that falls short of this theoretical benchmark suffers from "market failure," to use the term that economist Francis Bator and others used.[9] The policy implication is that government can correct a "market failure" by reallocating resources as indicated by theoretical models.

The implicit assumption in such analyses is that the government is an omniscient, benevolent dictator. It has sufficient information to allocate resources efficiently (omniscience), it has the desire to allocate resources efficiently (benevolence), and it has the power to do so (dictatorship). In the academic literature, this approach to policy analysis has been referred to as the planner's problem. The planner is the omniscient, benevolent dictator who must find the solution to the optimal allocation of resources, and economists who frame a planner's problem always conclude by showing the planner's solution. While this approach has been criticized,[10] it remains generally accepted in academic economics. Economists routinely identify inefficiencies in resource allocation and show what the government needs to do to correct the inefficiency without analyzing whether the government has sufficient information and the right incentives to actually accomplish what the analyst recommends. An analysis of government decision-making as Mises suggests shows that the government is not omniscient, it is not benevolent, and it is not a dictator.

The government is not omniscient. Often, government decision-makers do not have the necessary information to implement the recommended policy. Economists assume that policymakers know people's preferences, that external costs can be measured, and that, in general, policymakers can identify the optimal allocation of resources in real life that economists have identified in theory.

However, policymakers can never obtain much of this information. As Hayek noted, the information necessary to optimally allocate resources is decentralized, and often only the person who has this information can use it effectively.[11] When they undertake policy analysis, economists tend to ignore Hayek's insight that policymakers cannot acquire or act on this decentralized knowledge.

The government is not benevolent. Policymakers consider their own interests when making decisions and formulating policies. This point has also been well established but widely ignored. For example, political economist William Niskanen developed a well-known and frequently cited model of bureaucracy that concludes that government bureaucrats attempt to maximize their budgets,[12] and as a result, political leaders inefficiently allocate excessive resources to them. Interest-group models of government illustrate how politicians and interest groups, following the incentives of the political process, inefficiently allocate resources.[13] Yet, too often policy analysts assume that those in government set aside their own interests to further the public interest.

The government is not a dictator, in the sense of being omnipotent. Even dictatorships must rely on a power structure to keep the dictator in power, so people with political power must provide benefits to their supporters to maintain that power. This fact is true whether dictators support their cronies or whether elected officials provide special-interest benefits to the majority coalition that elects them.[14] One individual, even a "dictator," cannot unilaterally make and enforce government decisions because everyone in power relies on a group of supporters to maintain that power, regardless of whether it is a group of cronies in a dictatorship or a majority in a democracy. The concept of gridlocked government is common in an analysis of democracy precisely because there is no dictator, but rather a political process that requires the support of many to pass any policy. The same is true of every government that has been called a dictatorship: no government can operate without a group of cronies to support the dictator's position and power. Government decisions are the result of a collective decision-making process that always requires the support of many people; they are not made by a singular entity, even in a dictatorship.

The government is not an omniscient, benevolent dictator. Understanding the way the government works requires understanding the information limitations government decision-makers face, the incentive structure that may push them to act against the public interest, and the collective process by which a large group makes government decisions instead of a dictator unilaterally imposing them. Analyzing the claim that various political and economic systems are all variants of liberalism and cronyism requires setting aside the myth of the omniscient, benevolent dictator. The next several chapters examine various political and economic systems to see how they actually work in practice rather than how they might ideally work in theory.

CHAPTER 2:
CAPITALISM

C APITALISM IS AN economic system based on private ownership, the protection of property rights, rule of law, and voluntary exchange. Capitalism is the economic component of Locke's liberalism,[1] which starts with the concept of self-ownership. Because people own their labor, they come to own property when they combine their labor with unowned resources. Property ownership implies that owners can use their property as they want, as long as they do not violate others' rights. They can sell or trade it, give it away, or lend it to others. Transfers of economic resources under capitalism occur through voluntary agreement and voluntary exchange, and because people have the right to decide how they will use their property, they may make any exchanges they want to. The role of the government in a capitalist economy is to protect individuals' rights.

While Locke offered a moral foundation for a capitalist economy based on self-ownership, this moral foundation is not necessary for capitalism to be understood as the economic component of liberalism. Capitalism is economic liberalism because it protects property rights, because interpersonal interactions are voluntary, and because it permits voluntary exchanges as long as they do not violate others' rights.

Modern capitalist economies do not meet this ideal description of capitalism because they have incorporated elements of coercion into economic activity. Labor laws, such as the minimum wage law and professional licensing requirements, restrict labor transactions; taxes and transfers take property from some people to give to others; and the government restricts or prohibits many types of exchanges. The government requires that automobiles have seat belts, air bags, and more; it restricts the sale of prescription drugs and prohibits the sale of many recreational drugs; and it heavily regulates industries ranging from air travel to banking. The government heavily taxes some businesses and subsidizes others. Through these activities, capitalism has been combined with other economic systems, perhaps for the public interest, perhaps not. Government interventions to protect people's economic well-being fall under the heading of progressivism. Government direction of economic activity falls under the heading of industrial policy. Government ownership of economic activity—electric utilities, roadways, and schools are common examples—is socialism.[2]

Is a pure form of capitalism, with fully private ownership of property and in which people interact only through mutual consent, possible? Two writers who have made persuasive cases that a purely voluntary society is possible are David Friedman and Murray Rothbard.[3] Rothbard uses a liberal moral foundation based on Locke's ideas to argue that such a political and economic system is not only possible but is the only ethical way in which to organize a society.[4] Friedman, on the other hand, eschews Rothbard's deontological framework and makes the case for pure capitalism on utilitarian grounds. Not every liberal thinker agrees. Hayek and Ayn Rand, for example, see a role for government in providing legal services in a liberal order.[5]

History shows that when nations have adopted capitalism, they have grown and prospered. Throughout history, everywhere in the world, countries that have adopted capitalist economies have grown wealthy, while those that have not have remained poor.[6] Fifty years ago, China and India were among the poorest nations on Earth. Since the 1990s, as both have moved toward capitalism, they have had the highest economic growth rates in the world. While it is true that all capitalist economies have had some government presence, the evidence indicates that the smaller that presence, and the more the government uses its power to protect individuals' rights rather than to tax and regulate economic activities, the more prosperity those economies have enjoyed. Economists James Gwartney and Robert Lawson measure the degree to which economies have capitalist institutions, calling it "economic freedom."[7] Their Economic Freedom of the World index analyzes five broad areas: size of government, legal system and property rights, sound money, freedom to trade internationally, and levels of regulation. A vast literature shows that the more economic freedom a country enjoys, the higher that country's GDP and economic growth.

There are many reasons why people have argued that there are social benefits from government intervention in the economy, ranging from protecting the liberal order to enacting progressive reforms to enhancing people's economic well-being. The chapters that follow argue that regardless of the motivations for these interventions, or whether they are, on balance, beneficial, they inevitably lead to cronyism. Capitalism is the economic manifestation of liberalism; the alternatives are economic and political systems that are variants of cronyism.

CHAPTER 3:
SOCIALISM

Socialism is an economic system in which the citizenry owns and controls the means of production. In practice, socialism has meant government ownership, but cooperative ownership in which the workers at a firm are its owners is another variant. In the socialist economy typified by the former Soviet Union, state planners directed their subordinates and factory administrators to meet a certain output level based on a predetermined national plan. Because socialism does not publicly recognize private property rights in the means of production, political connectedness in socialist systems is rewarded with powerful positions that grant monopoly use of specific resources, elite class status, and access to the few rare luxuries that exist in economies of extreme scarcity. Because government leaders grant privileges to the people who have connections to those with political power, those without privilege try to gain favor with those with power in order to procure the benefits they see going to those with connections.

Socialism results in cronyism because it incentivizes individuals to compete for influence among a privileged class instead of competing for business by satisfying consumer demands. Examples of rent-seeking, clientelism, corruption, and political privilege abound in socialist economies the world over, including in the Soviet Union, China, Cuba, and North Korea. The forms of cronyism that emerged from these socialist economies are remarkably similar despite vast differences in the countries' geography, history, and culture.

The former Soviet Union provides a wealth of information on the day-to-day functioning of a centralized command economy. Recently released Soviet archives have prompted a flood of academic inquiries that compare the theoretical vision of socialism with the daily realities of the world's largest and oldest socialist economy. Because these countries shared similar political and economic systems, many tendencies detailed in these extensive Soviet archives have reportedly taken place in pre-reform socialist China as well as in the modern socialist economies of North Korea and Cuba, although access to these other countries' records is more limited. Additionally, China,[1] North Korea,[2] and Cuba[3] have been heavily influenced by Soviet socialism and Soviet advisers. Thus, an analysis of Soviet records can help to provide an institutional context for the similar phenomena that occurred in many socialist societies but that have not been comprehensively studied because of limited access to reliable data.

The Soviet internal reports paint a picture of a socialist economy that was "planned" in name only.[4] Despite the careful calculations and best intentions of Gosplan, the state planning committee in the Soviet Union, the outcomes of economic directives barely resembled the spirit of the planners' wishes by the time the responsible manager made a decision on the factory floor. This discrepancy between plans and reality created short-ages in supply chains and a scarcity of consumer goods. These institutional flaws in socialist systems led to the development of two major forms of cronyism: cronyism among state bodies and cronyism between state officials and nonstate officials. Members of the state-protected class, called the *nomenklatura* in the Soviet Union, *may-imbes* in Cuba, the *chuang-yü* in China, and the "nucleus class" in North Korea, leveraged their state-granted privileges to control resources and enforce the law in order to procure the inputs that they needed beyond their official supply to produce the state-set quotas for their factories. Members of the nonprotected classes petitioned the state elites for extra rations, leniency in law enforcement, and luxury goods by offering them bribes and favors. Because certain members of socialist society had greater access to the bureaucratic channels and centers of authority that signed off on these deci-sions, these people were able to amass relative personal riches, or at least avoid being sentenced to a work camp, by pulling on the strings of influence.

The structure of economic socialism leads public offi-cials to leverage influence and power within the state apparatus to obtain the resources needed to do their jobs. The size and scope of the Soviet Union prevented the general secretary and his small Politburo from dedicat-ing enough time and scrutiny to each economic proposal. In this complex system of planning and management that Soviet leaders created to lift this burden from the high-est offices, the "smaller dictators" that headed subordi-nate planning offices had to balance the interests of their own industries with the national priorities sent from the Politburo and the needs of connected industries.[5] The absence of a functioning price system eliminated the incentives that normally guide economic production to direct scarce resources to their highest-valued uses. Uncertainty about the quality and quantity of incoming inputs led to widespread hoarding and underreporting of inventories at every step of production and every level of employment, which only exacerbated the problem.

Along each link in the chain of command, the body or department attempted to squeeze as many resources from its subordinates as possible while returning as few supplies to its supervisors as possible. The price of not meeting a yearly quota could be excruciatingly high; an unfortunate manager who was unable to produce the required output could be demoted, sent to a work camp, or even sentenced to death for his "incompetence." Without a way to properly assess supply and demand, state managers resorted to alternative, extralegal methods to game the system in order to procure the resources they needed.

One way for public officials to procure required resources and avoid retribution was to gain influence with high-level sources of state power, and Soviet records detail several instances of political favoritism trumping economic intuition in economic planning. For instance, a 1931 crisis in grain allocation resulted in burgeoning civil unrest throughout the agricultural regions.[6] Although the Politburo was resolute in its dedication to the ratified plan regardless of the changes in conditions, regional leaders felt pressure from the farmers they oversaw—who were becoming weak and unruly because the short-sighted, export-driven agricultural policy with which they were saddled left precious few nutrients for their own families. The cruel calculus of the state plan forced regional leaders to make the difficult decision to either meet their grain production quotas for export to urban centers and abroad while ignoring their constituents' need for food, or ignore the unrealistic directives and face harsh punishment. These leaders furiously petitioned Stalin and his closest advisers for a reduction in their quotas. Stalin intervened and reduced quotas for the regions whose leaders were most aggressive in lobbying for a change, while raising quotas for other regions that were not as well-represented to make up for the loss. The less prominent officials who did not court favor with the higher echelons of the Soviet leadership would not be so fortunate as to have the rules rewritten for their benefit.

Economic policy in the Soviet Union was inseparable from the winds of political influence. For instance, political influence dictated public policy in the Soviet research and development industry.[7] Engineers who spent time lobbying and building up a political reputation were more likely to be selected for lucrative state grants and fellowships than colleagues who were not as familiar with the political apparatus. More senior state officials in all industries routinely sacrificed unimportant Soviet officials as "fall guys."[8] Likewise, public officials who openly questioned state policies found that their careers ended abruptly. The institutional structure of socialism therefore encourages state officials to dedicate much of their energy toward building relationships with superiors while casting blame on subordinates and toeing the official line with minimal—if any—objections. Rather than promoting a culture where government officials consider the benefits and costs of different policy options and promote employees based on merit, socialism creates a toxic environment that rewards undesirable character traits, as Hayek noted when he explained why the worst get on top in such systems.[9] Under socialism, people get ahead through their connections—cronyism—rather than through productivity.

Civilians in socialist economies live austere lives of extreme scarcity and uncertainty. State distribution centers provide notoriously meager rations to nonelite members of society and offer no legal channels by which people can procure more. As economic conditions worsen and vital food supplies start to dry up from state storehouses, the issue of obtaining sustenance becomes one of life or death. Facing these dramatic conditions, citizens of socialist countries have incentives to turn to prohibited activities in order to avoid starvation. Over time, members of the nonprivileged classes begin to exploit the institutional weaknesses inherent in socialism in order to survive. The abolition of a natural price system substitutes time and influence for natural market prices. Goods flow to those who can wait in line for hours, those who have many family members with whom to share rations, and, despite the stated socialist values of egalitarianism and classlessness, those who have personal connections with the officials who distribute resources. For instance, Cuban citizens who are fortunate enough to have personal relationships with their neighborhood *jefe de servicios*, or chief of services, who is responsible for distributing daily necessities to nonelite workers, receive extra resources and high-quality rarities that their less-connected neighbors never see.[10] Collective farm authorities in socialist

China functioned in a similar way; during agricultural famines, a person's relationship and past tribute to his or her farm authority could spell the difference between life and death.[11] Left with no alternatives, nonprotected members of socialist societies soon learn that the surest way to receive necessary resources is to generate influence among elite state officials who control access to "the people's" property.

The tensions that exert pressure on socialist systems have to be resolved through some means. Because the formal procedures are unworkable, informal practices develop to facilitate life within socialist societies. Two norms emerged to overcome the problems of state coordination and consumer scarcity in the Soviet Union.[12] When resources could not be procured through legal channels, Soviet citizens relied on the *blat* system of obtaining favors through personal influence to do daily business. A *tolkach*, or "smooth operator," facilitated the blat. He would function as an intermediary between the informal buyers and sellers of a resource, in addition to traveling and procuring more influence around the countryside.

Usually, a tolkach had a formal position at the factory he represented, but occasionally tolkachi became so successful at their trade that they acted as full-time tolkachi and served several clients at once. While the blat and tolkachi system certainly helped to float normally unattainable goods on the black market and therefore improved the living standards of nonconnected people, the state used favoritism and influence to determine the initial allocation of the privileges to control resources. The prevalence of blat and tolkachi shows how a welfare-enhancing informal order was ultimately predicated upon state privilege and disproportionately benefited a protected class of society. The collapse of the Soviet Union dramatically reduced the prevalence of blat and tolkachi in everyday life.

Similar phenomena emerged in the socialist systems of Cuba and China. A reciprocal exchange of personal favors, known as *socialismo* or *amiguismo* in Cuba, pre-dated the socialist system in that country but took on a new importance after the rise of the command economy.[13] In China, this informal network of favoritism and influence peddling was called *guanxi* or *ganqing* and was like-wise a critical part of life under socialism.[14] Individuals who received state power to control resources were in a position to make a significant personal profit by charging for access to the stockpiles. Because socialismo plays a prominent role in Cuban state planning and resource management to this day, even mundane economic planning becomes highly political and dependent upon personal relationships. State employees in the education and health care fields find themselves devoting more time to cultivating political relationships and less time to providing services to people that need them.[15]

In China, guanxi and *caigouyuan*, the Chinese equivalent of tolkachi, were likewise necessary developments that helped individuals function in a dysfunctional economic system. Although the practice of guanxi formed the "fabric of Chinese society" before the rise of the socialist Chinese state, it would be "a mistake to think that the fabric [was] the same" after the socialist system's formation.[16] The adoption of socialism in China fundamentally changed the institution of guanxi from a system predicated upon a myriad of voluntary informal connections to one that is "funneled through a single, state-approved local official" who receives the lion's share of the benefits. China's liberalization has tempered the widespread use of guanxi to procure necessary resources, but the practice continues in some sectors because the state still holds considerable sway over economic affairs.

Being designated as a member of the nomenklatura, mayimbes, chuang-yü, or nucleus class is a great privilege. When asked the survey question, "What is the best way to get ahead in North Korea?," 80 percent of North Korean refugees responded, "being a member of the officialdom."[17] By being granted the ability to control resources, regional and industrial leaders became a part of a tiny elite class. Historical records show that the government sometimes literally auctioned off to the highest bidder access to an elite state job in the Soviet Union. In North Korea, even the law is open to the highest bidder; convicted black market operatives could avoid a stint in the gulag by paying police to look the other way.[18] Bribery is a constant presence in socialist systems because public officials are the only individuals who have the privilege of accessing state resources. They are able to siphon off state rations and sell them for a profit on the black market before reporting inventories and submitting resources to the next step of production. Indeed, membership in this elite class in a socialist society provided a substantial advantage in navigating the systems of blat and socialismo; it is always preferable to be the bribee rather than the briber.

In addition to the ongoing profit opportunity afforded to the nomenklatura, mayimbes, chuang-yü, and nucleus class, leaders routinely rewarded these elite classes for their loyalty to the socialist state with luxurious gifts. In the Soviet Union, high-ranking officials received gifts of automobiles and single-family apartments that had all but vanished after the revolution.[19] Members of this class were vastly wealthier than their unfortunate fellow comrades, and their children were much more likely to attend an elite university than the children of collective farmers were.[20] Competition for admission to universities was fierce in the Soviet Union, with less than 20 percent of a high school graduating class accepted each year. In Cuba, recent budget pressures have prompted the state to slash public education for all schools but those attended by the children of the party elite, such as the Lenin School in Havana.[21] The extreme educational privilege granted to the children of the elite effectively creates a solid class system in which upward mobility is severely restricted.

Politicians in socialist China gave urban state employees priority access to education, health care, and public housing, while rural collective farmers lived in abject poverty.[22] During food shortages in the Soviet Union, the authorities placed state employees and political elites at the top of the list for food rations; peasants and collective farmers had to fend for themselves for sustenance.[23] In the 1970s, public officials in the country of Georgia participated in an "active competition" that *Pravda*, the official newspaper of the Central Committee of the Communisit Party of the Soviet Union, could only describe as "truly Tsarist" to see which official could embezzle the most state resources to build a personal mansion on public land.[24] Rather than eradicating social classes, socialism institutionalizes and protects the state court while siphoning resources from its subjects and charging them for the privilege of access.

Despite the considerable benefits afforded to individuals working within the Soviet state and the unsustainability of strictly centralized planning, archived records demonstrate that top Soviet officials disliked and desperately tried to eliminate the rampant corruption that saturated socialist society. In stark contrast to mixed economies, where cronyism is an intentional tool that political leaders use to induce industrialists to conform to the state's dictates, cronyism in socialist economies tends to be a costly unintended consequence. Corruption imposes much higher costs on an economy than taxation.[25] This "branching out" of interests within the Soviet planning apparatus was a fact of life that party officials only acknowledged in private correspondence. On the ground, average people navigated this web of connections and influence daily with the help of informal norms like blat and tolkachi that permeated the system. In secret correspondence to his closest councilors, Stalin privately despaired about his comrades' lack of revealed devotion to true socialist ideals as they scrambled to line their own pockets well before those of the state.[26]

High planners in the Soviet Union, Cuba, China, and North Korea all attempted to implement numerous anti-corruption edicts that encouraged whistle-blowing and ramped up punishments for corruption, but these initiatives were, perhaps unsurprisingly, either overwhelmingly ignored or selectively enforced. Despite their best efforts to create "socialist man" through education, propaganda, and state force, even the most ideologically dedicated socialists succumbed to the unavoidable forces of self-interest. The Soviet Union, with the extreme control it exercised over its citizens' lives, could not prevent cronyism from gripping every area in which the state intervened. Its example illustrates how government intrusion in economic affairs creates conditions under which individuals must divert energy away from productive activities like cost-cutting and improving production processes and toward destructive political competition in order to survive. In this way, the socialism of the Soviet Union, Cuba, China, and North Korea moved these countries' economies away from the positive-sum game that characterizes liberal capitalist economies and embraced the negative-sum game that permeates crony systems.

CHAPTER 4:
COMMUNISM

C OMMUNISM IS AN economic system characterized by communal ownership and production.
There is some overlap between the way the terms
"socialism" and "communism" are used, and the definitions used here are intended only to clarify the present
discussion, not to argue that other definitions are wrong.
Socialism, as discussed in the previous chapter, refers to
state ownership and control of the means of production,
whereas communism refers to communal ownership and
production as characterized by Karl Marx's statement,
"From each according to his ability, to each according to
his needs!"[1] Under communism, the community's production is shared among its members, as in the communal
farms in China and the *kibbutzim* in Israel. Like socialism
and unlike liberalism, communism is predicated upon a
central structure of economic command that is singularly
entrusted with allocating resources and making economic
decisions. Because of this centralized command structure,
communist societies fall prey to the forces of cronyism
and influence-peddling as commune members without
economic power curry favor with commune leaders that
control access to resources. The economic problems with

communism are well documented and widely understood, but the interpersonal problems of cronyism, clientelism, and influence-peddling are less well represented in the academic literature. The experiences of communal agriculture in post–World War II China and the kibbutzim of Israel provide good examples of how and why cronyism emerges from communist structures.

Agricultural communes in China, or "people's communes," had deep philosophical roots in Mao Zedong's disastrous push for collectivized industrialization, the Great Leap Forward. These communes had three levels of incremental authority and size: local production teams of around 25 households, production brigades of around 200 households, and entire communes of around 2,600 households. At the height of their power, commune leaders possessed the sole authority to oversee all facets of everyday life, including collective mess halls, communal sewing and garment capabilities, and even obligatory prekindergarten nurseries and education facilities that separated children from their parents.[2] Each level of authority offered political leaders, commonly referred to as "cadres," opportunities to skim the commune's resources for personal gain.

There were myriad problems with the distribution system of Chinese agricultural communes.[3] Because of their privileged positions within the state apparatus, cadres were often privy to information that their constituents were not. For this reason, it was common for cadres to suppress information about extra ration coupons that they would either steal for themselves or sell to the highest bidder. Similarly, cadres' price-setting authorities led to cronyist price discrimination that was outlawed on paper but practiced very widely around the country.

Seen as the purest embodiment of the communist ideal, people's communes were subject to various reforms in an effort to enhance productivity during their existence from 1958 until the mid-1980s. Throughout this thirty-year period, higher political authorities instructed cadre leaders to transfer the locus of power from the local level to the township and regional levels before finally returning political power to local hands following the liberalization reforms of Deng Xiaoping in 1978.[4] Following these liberalization efforts, people's communes could allocate private property rights from their communal land and tie incomes to value creation under the "responsibility system" of 1980. Despite the handful of conditions that the central government placed on these new rights and a spattering of indignant opposition from the most ideologically dedicated commune members, by 1981, the vast majority of communes had voluntarily adopted the responsibility reforms.[5] Additionally, the liberal-minded government of the late 1970s and early 1980s took serious steps to reverse the traditions of widespread cronyism. The leadership in post-Deng China combated institutional cronyism through a public media campaign that emphasized the virtues of whistleblowing and integrity in public service and through the creation of a Central Discipline Inspecting Commission that rooted out corruption and limited cadres' abilities to enrich themselves through the public coffers.[6]

As economic intuition would suggest, the years of greatest productivity for the people's communes occurred when power was decentralized and linked with accountability.

Accountability was embodied by reforms that paid commune members according to the value that they created rather than according to the arbitrary judgment of a cadre leader. After Chinese communes moved from a system characterized primarily by government privilege and cronyism to a system that integrated the liberal principles of property rights, accountability, and voluntary exchange, these communities became more prosperous and competitive. In spite of the few vestiges of cadre power that remained after the 1980 reform, economic growth in people's communes reduced absolute poverty and increased vertical mobility.[7] Additionally, these reforms largely diminished cadre leaders' and affiliated parties' abilities to enrich themselves at their constituents' expense. The returns to private entrepreneurship in rural communes that adopted reform efforts far outstrip the corresponding returns to political privilege.[8] It simply does not pay as much to be a crony in a more liberal, market economy.

The tendency of communist systems to devolve into cronyism largely stems from a lack of accountability of a leadership that is not personally bound to its constituents beyond what public duty requires. Recent inquiries into the natures of governance and morality suggest that shared moral systems can act as a "glue" that binds planners with those for whom they are planning and therefore reduces the tendency to defect from the public good. For instance, moral psychologist Jonathan Haidt suggests that the common moral dimensions of popular religions lower the transaction costs of interacting with other believers and therefore contribute to social harmony.[9] This finding would suggest that a communist system fundamentally grounded in religion and nationality, like the collective agricultural communities or *kibbutzim* in Israel, would be less vulnerable to the downfalls of communism that plagued the experiments in China's secular, disparate communities. Indeed, the kibbutz arrangement has outlasted all other modern attempts at communal agriculture and has avoided some of the more violent missteps of China's state communes; however, these cultural institutions have not been strong enough to completely eliminate the human propensity to take advantage of an easily exploitable system when given the opportunity to do so.

Despite the advantages that kibbutzim enjoy by virtue of a shared moral matrix and cultural identity, communal agriculture in Israel is susceptible to the same problems of cronyism, corruption, and clientelism that wracked other communes that lacked any shared values. The early kibbutz experiment that blossomed from the efforts of a handful of radical idealists in the 1920s and 1930s slowly wilted as the leaders aged and became more protective of their power.[10] In spite of the strict tenure limits that the informal norm of *rotatzia* ostensibly enforced, charismatic kibbutz leaders held onto power for dynasties that lasted for up to half a century. The executive leader rewarded subordinate office holders for their allegiance with increased power, tenure, and luxurious gifts like cars and private flats, while rank-and-file members had to make do with their meager communal rations. For most of their existence, Israeli kibbutzim have not been self-sufficient but rather dependent on critical external financial support from Jewish and Israeli institutions.[11] It is perhaps not surprising, then, that kibbutz elites have consistently dominated the national Israeli political scene despite comprising only 3 percent of the Israeli population.[12] Additionally, the incentives of the kibbutz prompt high-skilled workers to seek better-paying opportunities elsewhere. One study found that the kibbutz redistribution scheme that moves wealth from value creators to political insiders is associated with an exodus of high-skilled workers from the communes.[13] These problems have been percolating among small kibbutz networks for decades and have started to take their toll.

In fact, much of the modern academic literature on the kibbutzim discusses the "crisis" that has been gradually undermining the harmony and productivity of kibbutzim over many silent decades.[14] Even scholars who generally support the concept of communal agriculture and are committed to the kibbutzim's success as a proof of concept for socialism correctly identify the emergence of a self-interested political elite as a primary weakness of the kibbutz arrangement while simultaneously pinning the blame of this outcome on the moderate liberalizing reforms that some kibbutzim have enacted in order to more correctly align value creation with compensation and entice the high-skilled laborers that are leaving the system to move back to their kibbutzim. At the same time, many of the reform proposals that these scholars offer, primarily a return to vertical centralization, are likely to only further aggravate the problems. To engender successful reform, the kibbutzim must emulate the successful reforms of the Chinese people's communes by diminishing the amount of rents that can be seized through political allocation and increasing the number of avenues through which all commune members can offer and trade value.

The successful reforms of agricultural communism in China and the recent reforms of the kibbutzim in Israel that decentralized power structures and linked leadership with accountability demonstrate how aligning incentives toward productive value creation and away from unproductive cronyism leads to sustainable prosperity. As communist systems continue to modernize by adapting the liberal values that are critical to the development of a free and prosperous society while retaining the communal principles that prompted their creation, these communes will come closer to eliminating the potential for abuses of power and biased resource allocation based on personal influence. However, as economist Peter Boettke notes with reference to the Soviet Union, movements toward liberalism will have limited success because the lingering vestiges of communism leave the door open to cronyism.[15]

CHAPTER 5:
FASCISM

ASCISM, THE POLITICAL and economic system of Germany and Italy between the world wars, has sometimes been characterized as a capitalist economy ruled by an authoritarian government. An examination of how the system actually worked shows that political connections ultimately determined economic success in fascist Germany. Those with connections prospered while those without lost their businesses, sometimes because of the tilted playing field of cronyism, but sometimes through out-and-out confiscation that transferred economic resources to the control of cronies.

The rise of fascism in Germany in the 1930s was a result of the economic uncertainties and nationalistic upwelling of its weary populace after the collapse of the Weimar Republic. Adolf Hitler channeled the popular rage against the humiliation of the Versailles treaty and the anxieties of a nation that faced a 30 percent unemployment rate into developing and implementing a philosophy of total deference to the good of the nation-state. To make the Nazi vision a reality, the Third Reich exerted unprecedented control over Germans' private and economic affairs. The government implemented the actualization of this vision, the Four Year Plan, in 1936, with Hermann Göring as its head. The government thrust scores of new price controls, quotas, and licensing regulations at many areas of economic activity.[1] In some industries, transactions could not legally occur until a government oversight body approved them.[2] The government's growing role in the economy created an incentive for businessmen and special interests to cultivate relationships with powerful party officials who could bend or rewrite the rules to their favor. Economic and political favoritism in the Third Reich was both institutionalized, through direct legislation, and informal. As a result, cronyism was widely prevalent in fascist Germany.

The Nazi vision of economic policy discarded the virtues of competitive value creation, consumer sovereignty, and comparative advantage and replaced them with a political economy dictated by party objectives, political favoritism, and military production. The economic goals of Nazi planners prioritized rearmament, recovery, and national self-sufficiency, or autarchy.[3] These goals frequently aligned with the interests of established German industrialists, and the industrialists' political allies tailored policies for their need to ensure the compliance and support of this important interest group. In a 1927 memorandum to wealthy German industrialists, Hitler is explicit in his vision of public-private cooperation in economic activity: "The decisive factor in economic conflict in this world has never yet rested in the relative skill and know-how of the various competitors, but rather in the might of the sword they could wield to tip the scales for their business and hence their lives."[4] Hitler and his economic planners proceeded to use the sword of the Nazi state to tip the scales for the business people who were loyal to the Nazi party and its mission.

Cronyism in fascist Germany revolved around membership in and influence with the Nazi party.[5] The Nazi allegiance to the party line was like a currency that was traded through networks of political power. Nazi party officials rewarded members of the business community who were loyal party members with government positions and regulatory authority. It was not the raw economic power of the protected German industrialists that solidified their privileged status, but rather the connections they established with powerful party leaders. The Nazis rewarded loyalty to their party handsomely; German firms that were connected to the Nazi party through donations or membership in 1933 outperformed non-politically connected firms by 5 to 8 percent that year.[6] Over time, the value of political connections to the Nazi party grew significantly as the state either regulated nonconnected firms out of business or seized them outright.

The businesses with the most influence with the Nazi government received the most economic protection and assistance. For instance, Carl Duisberg, a cofounder and top executive of the chemical company I. G. Farben, gave significant campaign contributions to the Nazi party before and after its ascension to power.[7] These early bets paid significant dividends to Duisberg's company, as the Nazi party elevated I. G. Farben to the status of protected company within the Nazi regime. The policies of rearmament and autarchy meshed well with I. G. Farben's interests as one of Germany's largest synthetic petroleum producers. In addition, the enactment of Göring's Four

Year Plan created several government bodies that were responsible for planning and investment in the petroleum industry. The government awarded three I. G. Farben executives—E. R. Fischer, Karl Krausch, and Heinrich Bütefisch—top positions in these state regulatory agencies.[8] These executives were therefore able to steer government policy to align with their company's interests.[9]

These positions helped I. G. Farben to procure government contracts and eliminate its competitors. In order to ramp up oil production for the rearmament effort, the Ministry of Economics significantly subsidized I. G. Farben's process of hydrogenating synthetic fuel. Krausch was the administrator of the subsidization plan in the Raw Materials and Foreign Exchange staff and directed 70 percent of the subsidy money to I. G. Farben.[10] The party denied I. G. Farben's competitor, Ruhrchemie, subsidization of its superior hydrogenation process because it did not have the same political connections. Economic policies like these enriched the Nazi party's political allies at the expense of both their competitors and increased efficiency gains from competition.

One of the most ubiquitous practices of cronyism in Nazi Germany was the institutionalization of the existing trade cartels that predated the Third Reich. Rather than creating a new bureaucratic entity to rein in market competition, economic regulators took advantage of the existing cartels as a vehicle to enact their desired policies.[11] In 1933, the Ministry of Economics issued a decree that required all firms to join a trade cartel. This rule benefited both the planners and the cartel members; existing members of the cartels benefited from reduced price competition from smaller competitors, while economic planners created a back door for indirectly regulating industries. As time passed, the planners delegated to the cartel leaders more and more regulatory power over their own industries.[12] The government rewarded promising party members with top executive positions in "private" companies, and it offered devoted Nazi businessmen government positions in one of the numerous regulatory agencies. By 1938, it was virtually impossible to distinguish the business interests from the party interests in the cartel hierarchy.[13]

In Nazi Germany, the cost of being a political outsider was extremely high. In addition to indirectly regulating nonconnected firms out of business, the Nazi state often directly seized the means of production and property from its political enemies, from Jewish Germans, and from conquered peoples. In 1938, the Third Reich passed a law that stripped Jewish Germans of all claims to property and businesses and seized these assets. The party distributed the spoils of this direct theft to its top members and their allies and relatives.[14] After the German military conquered an area, it passed decrees that limited the native population's ability to transact and run their businesses. In Bohemia-Moravia, large domestic firms had to appoint a native German to the board of directors in order to do business.[15] Regulations like this one effectively transferred ownership to connected German parties. These occurrences serve to illustrate how political influence trumped competition and value creation in Nazi economic policy.

One of the easiest ways to survive in business in Nazi Germany was to devote time and resources toward cozying up to powerful members of the Nazi party. Those who did not cultivate these relationships and those who the Nazi party placed on its enemy list found themselves deprived of their property, businesses, and livelihoods. The German economy suffered as a result; the party dedicated resources to the fulfillment of its objectives of militarization and self-sufficiency and diverted resources away from fulfilling consumer needs.[16] It was only after government intervention in economic affairs declined in West Germany following the end of the war that cronyism shrank, allowing businesses to refocus on fulfilling consumer needs rather than political whimsies.

CHAPTER 6:
CORPORATISM

ORPORATISM IS A political philosophy that espouses the association of people with common interests into corporate groups, or state-mandated associations that ostensibly represent the political interests of their members. The philosophical underpinnings of corporatism arose from the works of nineteenth-century Catholic theologians who wanted to develop a social system that would organize individuals into state-directed groups that would serve and work toward the good of the community.[1] Corporatism remained a theoretical concept until interest rekindled with the rise of state dictatorships in the early twentieth century. Since that time, several countries have exhibited corporatist tendencies for varying lengths of time, including Russia,[2] the United Kingdom,[3] Argentina,[4] Portugal,[5] and, most famously, fascist Italy. The formal institutionalization of national corporations is a way to align the incentives of state, employer, and labor interest groups with the goals of a nation-state.

The modern conception of corporatism is most commonly associated with Benito Mussolini's Italy and is a variant of fascism. Corporatism in fascist Italy was born out of Mussolini's desire to wed the efficiency of traditional market capitalism with the enlightened planning of a powerful state. After his ascension to power with the March on Rome in 1922, Mussolini initially allowed the established liberal economic regime to continue functioning without major interventions by the state. Frustrated by the uncontrolled outcomes of competitive production, in 1926 Mussolini enacted reforms that entrusted more power in economic planning to state agents. Mussolini's vision of state capitalism consisted of segmented corporate entities owned by private interests that were beholden to the state's goals.[6] Mussolini therefore aimed to rein in the undisciplined outcomes of competitive capitalism by blurring the lines between state and market. In consolidating and cartelizing entire structures of production under the hierarchy of an authoritative corporation, Mussolini's corporatism incentivized individuals to expend their energy navigating the numerous and confusing corporatist chains of command instead of developing productive ways to create value for consumers.

In practice, Italian corporatism did not significantly differ from traditional fascism and can accurately be considered a subset of fascism. Like fascism, corporatism prioritizes the good of the nation-state above all other considerations, including individual well-being. Mussolini was very clear about his vision for Italy when he wrote in his 1928 autobiography that

> the citizen in the Fascist State is no longer a selfish individual who has the anti-social right of rebelling against any law of the Collectivity. The Fascist State with its corporative conception

puts men and their possibilities into productive work and interprets for them the duties they have to fulfill.[7]

Corporatism is unique in its adoption of corporate organization to achieve state goals. In consolidating companies and interest groups under one corporate hierarchy, Mussolini hoped to eliminate the class and business conflicts that could emerge from traditional fascism and that would detract from the realization of his national goals.

A law passed in 1930 organized all existing firms into one of twenty-two official corporations that were represented on the National Council of Corporations and influenced by more powerful government agencies like the Istituto per la Ricostruzione Industriale (IRI) and the Istituto Mobiliare Italiano (IMI). While not owned by the government per se, these corporations operated according to directives set by agencies like the IRI and IMI, whose regulatory rules shielded the corporations from domestic competition.[8] In addition, the government significantly curtailed the right of association. The law prohibited private labor groups and employers' associations with the expectation that these state corporate bodies would serve the interests of both groups. Despite this expectation, business interests overwhelmingly dominated the newly established state labor courts, corporative agencies, and economic bureaus created to replace the old private system. Historian Roland Sarti argues that these state institutions allowed businesses to "enjoy the benefits of public support without having to accept the onus of effective public control."[9]

The corporate bodies developed their own networks of extensive internal bureaucracy to ensure compliance with state directives and to promote efficient operations. State administrative and regulatory bodies developed similar structures that operated through government channels. This system resulted in a complicated and redundant network of regulatory, administrative, consultancy, and legislative offices that rarely coordinated information and were sometimes completely unaware of the others' existence.[10] Combined with a lack of independent oversight, this system resulted in rampant corruption, patronage, and inefficiency. Reports flew out of city centers to the administrative offices in Rome complaining of the extortion and favoritism that Italian officials practiced. Government and corporate officials routinely awarded themselves and their friends with lucrative government contracts and confiscated property intended for the "Fatherland."[11] Additionally, the government selectively enforced regulations and informally fast-tracked business licenses for friends and relatives of the state licensors. For example, a retail licensing requirement in 1926 resulted in widespread clientelism and a burgeoning black market for highly valued business licenses.[12] Because the new law did not formally spell out the qualifications for licensing, licensors creatively interpreted the vague guidelines to primarily include personal connections and those whom they wanted to reward politically.

Academics and journalists around the world applauded Mussolini's development of Italian corporatism. These intellectuals commended the bold Italian experiment for combining the best aspects of state planning with the best aspects of competitive capitalism.[13] They believed that this form of guided capitalism could correct market excesses and eliminate wasteful competition while still providing the efficiency of a market economy.

This enthusiasm for corporatism proved to be premature. Within a few years of its introduction, the corporatist model broke down. Rather than making selfless decisions that benefited a corporation for the good of the nation, managers and workers made decisions according to their own self-interests. As a result, the Italian experiment with corporatism did not produce an efficient, integrated economic machine working toward the good of the country, as Mussolini envisioned, but rather a confusing and haphazard network of public and private administrative bodies that jostled each other for resources and power. Corporatism became another form of cronyism.

Other nations that have experimented with corporatism have fallen victim to the same fate, as corporatist systems tend to disintegrate soon after their formation. While contemporary governments rarely adopt corporatism in such a blatant manner as fascist Italy, the recent trend of bailing out failing companies is an example of corporatism in modern times. This practice sets a dangerous precedent and signals to business leaders that having political connections could be more valuable to their bottom lines than staying competitive in the marketplace and creating value for their customers. As traditional corporatism does, this modern corporatism distorts incentives and directs businesses into nonproductive activities and away from value-creating activities.

CHAPTER 7:
DESPOTISM

THE EASIEST POLITICAL system to analyze in the liberalism-cronyism framework is despotism, which is a clear form of cronyism. While at first it may appear that despots wield absolute power, despots are only able to remain in power as long as they have sufficient support to prevent their overthrow. Examples like Stalin and Castro notwithstanding, most despots remain in power for a relatively short time. Political scientist Milan Svolik has collected a data set of 738 autocrats who ruled from 1945 on, and the median tenure of those autocrats was 3.2 years.[1] Regardless of the political system, those with political power can maintain it only with support.[2] In democracies, maintaining this support means gaining a majority's support in elections. In autocracies, the support group is more limited. A military dictatorship obviously requires the support of the military, and those with economic power must always be content enough with the incumbent regime that they will not step up to finance the opposition. In a nondemocratic government, political power must be maintained by force, because there is no other way for people discontented with the incumbent regime to replace it. Those in power must therefore provide sufficient benefits to their supporters so that those supporters, or cronies, continue to back the incumbent regime rather than the opposition. Cronies can always shift their allegiance to the despot's opposition if the opposition makes them a better offer.

Political power under despotism is always tenuous. On the one hand, even if a substantial share of the population would prefer a change in leadership, most people will not become activists because of the threats that despots can hold over those who oppose them. On the other hand, if the opposition gains sufficient support that it appears likely that they could take power, the general population's allegiance can suddenly and unpredictably shift.[3] Thus, it is important for despots to reward their cronies in order to maintain power.

The cronyism necessary to support despotic governments is one of the reasons economists Daron Acemoglu and James Robinson cite for the poor economic performance such governments deliver.[4] Similarly, referring to the poor nations of Africa, Ghanaian economist and president of the Free Africa Foundation George Ayittey says, "African despots are loath to relinquish control or power. They would rather destroy their economies and countries than give up economic and political power. This power allows them to allocate or extract resources to build personal fortunes and to dispense patronage to buy political support."[5] That patronage is cronyism.

Despotism is a form of cronyism because despots need the support of cronies to remain in power, and cronies offer that support in exchange for the favors that the force of despotic government can provide them. Despite economic models that depict government as an omniscient, benevolent dictator, the ability of dictators to be impartially benevolent is limited because they must always benefit their cronies. If there is no advantage to being a crony, there is no reason for cronies to support the despot. Thus, despots must support their cronies to remain in power.

CHAPTER 8:
PROGRESSIVISM

P ROGRESSIVISM AROSE AS a political movement in the late 1800s in response to a rise in the concentration of economic power following the Industrial Revolution. Liberalism was the political ideology that sparked the American Revolution and remained at the foundation of American politics through the late 1800s. The government's role within this liberal ideology was to protect individual rights. As economic power became more concentrated in the late 1800s, that liberal ideology evolved so that Americans saw the government's role not as limited to protecting their rights, but also as protecting their economic well-being. This latter role is the ideology of progressivism.

Economists Terry Anderson and Peter Hill note the significance of the Supreme Court case *Munn v. Illinois* as a landmark progressive event, which they call "the birth of a transfer society."[1] That 1877 case allowed states to regulate the rates that grain elevators could pay for grain, opening the door for government regulation of various aspects of commerce. The Sherman Antitrust Act, passed in 1890, prohibited business activities that limited competition, allowing the government to dissolve cartels and regulate or break up monopolies. The Pure Food and Drug Act of 1906 limited the sale of certain medicines, required labeling to be accurate, and created the federal inspection of meat packaging operations. In the twenty-first century, we take regulations like these for granted, along with professional licensure requirements for many occupations and government regulation of many products and businesses.

Economic historian Robert Higgs argues that this progressive agenda came from a change in ideology in the late 1800s, after which people wanted the government to expand its powers to look out for their economic well-being in addition to protecting their rights.[2] In the twentieth century, the government responded to crises like wars and economic depression by expanding its budget and powers, ratcheting up its size as the progressive agenda grew. The government extended its regulatory oversight of economic activity to look out for people's economic well-being by supporting their incomes in addition to regulating commerce. Social Security, Medicare, Medicaid, food stamps, unemployment compensation, and a host of other wealth-transfer programs are designed to protect the economic well-being of many groups of citizens. These programs' existence shows the extent to which progressivism has become a part of the accepted political ideology in the twenty-first century. By the time of Lyndon Johnson's "Great Society" in the 1960s, the ideology of liberty—the idea that the government's role is to protect people's rights—had been transformed into the ideology of democracy, the idea that the government's role is to carry out the will of the people.[3]

The progressive ideology has been accepted even by

people who argue for limited government, when they support limited government using the argument that most people favor smaller government. This argument concedes that the government should carry out the will of the people, and a majoritarian government is not a liberal government. Under this reasoning, some mechanism must reveal the people's will, and that mechanism is representative democracy, where the people express their will through voting, lobbying, and financially supporting political candidates and their parties. Because politicians can keep their hold on power only with such support, progressivism leads to cronyism; politicians will meet people's demands to the extent that those people support them. With many competing groups all arguing that supporting their interests will further the public interest, it is unrealistic to expect a result other than cronyism.

Economist Mancur Olson argues that nations decline when interest groups become well-established in the political process so that firms gain more from their political connections than from their economic productivity.[4] In other words, cronyism leads to the decline of nations. Olson argues that a young political system will have weak political interest groups and political connections will not have developed to the point where businesses can count on favors from the government. When political interests are weak, entrepreneurial individuals have an incentive to engage in economically productive activity, which results in economic growth. This process creates the rise of nations, as Olson describes it. Over time, political interest groups grow and solidify, and they establish relationships with those who have government power. As they do, success increasingly comes from the ability to use political connections—from cronyism—rather than from the ability to engage in economically productive activity. When the power of political connections overwhelms the power of economic productivity, nations enter a decline.

Economist William Baumol suggests that the amount of entrepreneurial activity is roughly the same in every society. Societies prosper when the institutional framework is organized such that the payoff from economically productive activity is higher than the payoff from using political connections to get ahead.[5] Where political connections are more important, entrepreneurial individuals engage in political entrepreneurship to try to place themselves within the power elite, where they can prosper by taking from the productivity of others. Where poor institutions allow individuals to gain more wealth through political connections than through productive activity, people have less incentive to be productive and more incentive to seek profitable political connections, which generates cronyism and lower growth. Societies suffer when their institutional framework causes the payoff from using political connections to get ahead to exceed the payoff from economically productive activity that increases societal wealth.

The idea behind progressivism is that the government's role is to look out for people's economic well-being in addition to protecting their rights, but this system leads directly to government policies that favor some people at the expense of others. The earliest manifestations of progressivism in the late 1800s—regulating grain elevator prices, or establishing antitrust laws—were specifically designed to promote the interests of some at a cost to others. More modern programs like Social

Security, Medicare, and Medicaid do the same, and there is an ongoing debate about how much the beneficiaries of progressive programs should receive at the expense of those who pay for them. Regardless of these programs' good intentions, the object of progressivism is to use government force to provide economic benefits to some by imposing costs on others, which leads people to engage in political entrepreneurship to influence the government to favor them. Cronies benefit under this system, and those without strong political connections pay the cost.

CHAPTER 9:
MAJORITARIANISM

EMOCRACY IS NEARLY synonymous in popular usage with majority rule, with the idea that a democratic government should carry out the majority's will. However, the American Founders did not envision their new nation as a democracy in this sense. Rather, they deliberately designed the federal government to be insulated from popular opinion. If we take the idea of checks and balances and the separation of powers among the three branches of government seriously, those branches must have roughly the same power to check and balance each other. If they do, then the original design of the US government under the Constitution was one-sixth democratic. Let us explain.

Members of the judiciary are appointed by the president and confirmed by Congress, so there is no direct mechanism for popular opinion to influence them. Supreme Court justices are appointed for life, further insulating them from democratic pressures. State legislatures originally chose senators, so senators represented the interests of their states, were not subject to popular approval, and were not accountable to popular opinion. The Seventeenth Amendment, which specifies the direct election of senators, changed this system when it was ratified in 1913. Originally, only the members of the House of Representatives were chosen by popular vote. Representatives were to represent the interests of the people and senators were to represent the interests of state governments; however, with popular voting for both senators and representatives, the two groups now represent the same constituencies. The House of Representatives was the only part of the government designed to respond to the will of the people, however, and as half of one of the three branches, the Founders thus originally designed our government to be one-sixth democratic.

The electoral college chooses the president, and the Constitution has never specified how electors are chosen. The most common method in 1800 was for the state legislature to choose a state's electors.[1] The idea was that the electors would be better informed about the candidates than members of the general public would be, so the electors would nominate two candidates, at least one of whom had to be from a state other than the elector's. The Founders thought that, in general, this method of election would result in no candidate receiving an electoral majority, in which case the five top vote-getters would have their names forwarded to the House of Representatives, and the House would choose the president.[2] In other words, the electoral college would serve as a search committee to forward names to the House of Representatives, where the president would be selected. This process would insulate presidential selection from democratic pressures and insulate the president from the pressures of popular opinion. The system did not work as the Founders intended, however, and by the 1820s, most states had switched to the present system of popular voting for electors. However, the Constitution never has said, and still does not specify, how states must choose their electors.

It may sound anti-American to question the merits of the current conception of democracy, so it is worth emphasizing that the Founders did not originally design the government to be responsive to the will of the people. The federal government was one of limited and enumerated powers, and democracy was a mechanism for choosing who held those powers and for making it relatively easy to replace them if they abused their office and its powers.

The majoritarian vision of democratic government favors those who have the majority's support. A public-interest viewpoint might approve of favoring the poor, for example, or the working class, and might approve of imposing costs to pay for these favors on robber barons, or the rich, or those who smoke cigarettes. Nevertheless, when the government favors some groups over others, it incites political competition to be in a group that gets government favors and to avoid being in a group that pays for them. That competition leads to cronyism.

Nobody knows what popular opinion is before people express their opinions, which gives everyone an incentive to argue that their interests are congruent with popular opinion when the government operates under the political philosophy of majoritarianism. People have a strong incentive to argue for their own interests, but at best a weak incentive to argue for the public interest, and arguing for the public interest displaces an opportunity to argue for narrow individual interests. In this environment, economists Barry Weingast, Kenneth Shepsle, and Christopher Johnsen describe a government engaged in distributive politics, where people must try to join a group of cronies in order to receive their share.[3] Such behavior reinforces cronyism because gaining advantages in a democratic government requires others' support.

Recent work in the new institutional economics, including that of Douglass North, John Wallis, and Barry Weingast as well as that of Daron Acemoglu and James Robinson,[4] describes the poor institutions in which rising to the top of the income distribution depends on political power and connections rather than economic productivity. The reliance on connections is cronyism. Acemoglu and Robinson describe these institutions as extractive rather than inclusive,[5] so there is an advantage to being a crony who can extract benefits rather than engage in productive activity. Majoritarianism leads to cronyism.

CHAPTER 10:
ENVIRONMENTALISM

ENVIRONMENTALISM IS A broad social movement that is concerned with environmental protection, conservation, and sustainability. It may seem odd to include environmentalism in a book about political and economic systems, but in the twenty-first century, the goal of environmental protection drives a significant amount of public policy. In the context of liberalism, the government's role is to protect individual rights. Environmentalism often wants to extend similar governmental protections to other species and even to inanimate objects like lakes and sand dunes. Certainly the natural environment has value, but that value does not necessarily mean that bears, wolves, and sand dunes should be extended the same constitutional protections the government gives to people. Markets and property rights can protect valuable environmental amenities just as markets and property rights produce value in other goods and services.[1] The purpose of the present study is not to debate the issue of environmental protection, however, but to show how, when injected into the political process, environmentalism leads to cronyism.

Modern advocates of environmentalism can trace

their roots to diverse sources of inspiration, ranging from Rousseau's admiration for the "noble savage" to the Calvinist tradition of viewing nature as God's revelation of power to the American transcendental movement of Henry David Thoreau and Ralph Waldo Emerson.[2] Although the environmental movement is comprised of several different factions with varying emphases for reform, one unifying feature of the movement is that its advocates tend to place a higher value on environmental concerns than on economic progress. It is not surprising, then, that many environmental advocates are indifferent to, or even purposefully negligent of, the potential negative effects of their proposed reforms on economic prosperity. The philosophy of environmentalism and the philosophy of economic growth are fundamentally opposed to each other, and both philosophies' vocal supporters have been jockeying with each other for political dominance for the past century.[3] One reason that environmentalists and free market advocates are so opposed to each other is that environmentalists tend to advocate increased government intervention into economic matters, and many of the environmental policies the government has enacted have led to cronyism.

Environmentalists support many different kinds of government interventions to correct what they view as the inevitable excesses of market capitalism that contribute to environmental degradation. In particular, recent concerns about global climate change have increased the demands for environmental interventions in economic affairs. Examples of common environmental policies include environmental regulation, government subsidies to experimental energy alternatives, targeted tax incentives, selective taxation, and cap-and-trade proposals. Some of these policies, like government loan guarantees to "green" firms, provide clear examples of cronyism. Other policies, like environmental regulation, grant privileges to specific firms in a more subtle way. Although these policies are diverse in their approaches, they all share the common characteristic of putting government representatives in a position to choose the economic winners and losers. Modern environmental policy therefore resembles industrial policy in the sense that the government selects which firms should be favored under the law and which firms should be targeted for taxes and regulatory penalties. While environmental policies may begin with good intentions, recent experience in the United States with environmental interventions has shown that when placed in a position to distribute benefits to friends, associates, and political allies, government employees often succumb to this temptation.

The recent loan guarantee program from the Department of Energy (DOE) provides a clear-cut example of government cronyism in environmental policy. George W. Bush signed the program into law through the Energy Policy Act of 2005 and Barack Obama implemented the program and promoted it to the public as a necessary investment in America's green economy. The program's proponents argued that innovative ideas in alternative energy sources have a hard time attracting investor funds due to the high risk involved in these initiatives.[4] Advocates concluded that the government must step in to provide economic security for the necessary funds to enable the development of these critical technologies. A public loan guarantee, in which the government promises to assume a company's debt if it fails, is one way to provide security for risk-wary investors.

Although proponents justified the program on the grounds of financial necessity, the government did not distribute loan guarantees solely on the basis of merit. The Government Accountability Office raised multiple concerns about the inconsistency and arbitrariness of the DOE's administrative procedures in selecting the companies that would receive a public loan guarantee.[5] Closer examination reveals that the government did not primarily award the DOE loan guarantees to the kinds of small, innovative startups that traditionally have difficulty securing sufficient investment, but rather to large, established firms.[6] Additionally, 90 percent of the loan guarantees went to relatively low-risk power plants, many of which were already backed by large companies with sufficient financial resources.[7] This distribution of loan guarantees was contrary to the program's stated intent of supporting innovative technologies that are unable to obtain traditional financing. Some firms even "double dipped" into the public trough by receiving multiple loan guarantees through subsidiary companies.

What is more concerning, however, is that many of the loan guarantees appear to have been prioritized for firms with connections to the Obama administration. One of the most publicized examples of this kind of cronyism is the case of cylindrical solar panel manufacturer Solyndra. The Department of Energy extended a $535 million loan guarantee to Solyndra despite some staffers' lingering questions about the company's future profitability. Solyndra's political connections allowed the company to receive a grant despite shaky fiscal forecasts. One of

Solyndra's major investors, George Kaiser, contributed $50,000 to Obama's campaign efforts and helped to raise another $50,000 to $100,000 in donations.[8] Emails released by House Republicans in November 2011 show that Kaiser, who was a regular guest at the White House in the months before Solyndra was awarded the grant, was optimistic about the company's chances of securing a loan guarantee because he had won the favor of Secretary of Energy Steven Chu and Vice President Joe Biden. Although the administration denied that it granted the loan guarantee to Solyndra because of the firm's political connections, it is clear that the administration favored this company as a poster child of the program and that the firm did have personal connections to the administration—a clear case of cronyism. Internal communications reveal that the White House pressured the Office of Management and Budget behind the scenes to approve the necessary documentation for the loan guarantees in time for scheduled public appearances at the company by Vice President Biden and President Obama.

Although the Solyndra scandal is the most well-known scandal of the DOE loan guarantee program, this instance of cronyism is likely just the tip of the iceberg. One estimate suggests that the government awarded 70 to 80 percent of the loan guarantees to firms in which the primary investor or top executive financially supported Obama during his 2008 campaign.[9] A *Washington Post* investigation in February 2012 found that the government directed $3.9 billion in grants and loan guarantees to 21 companies with political connections to the Obama administration.[10] One former Obama fundraiser and DOE employee used his influence to procure $2.46 billion in benefits for his former venture capital firm, Vantage Point Venture Partners. Another venture capitalist turned Washington insider was working at the DOE while his former firm, General Catalyst, received $105 million in government support.

In addition to this direct kind of cronyism, environmental loan programs incentivize nonconnected firms to become politically connected to stay in business and remain competitive. For instance, an article in *Wired* magazine describes how electric car manufacturer Aptera Motors laid off 25 percent of its workforce so that it would have the resources to focus on procuring a DOE loan.[11] The remaining employees spent the bulk of their time navigating the myriad forms and processes that were necessary to procure government support. The incentives produced by government loan guarantees, grants, and subsidies remove resources from productive activities and direct them toward unproductive cronyism.

Another area in which cronyism manifests itself in environmental policy is regulation. Environmental regulation provides an excellent demonstration of economist Bruce Yandle's "bootleggers and Baptists" political model.[12] Contrary to the commonly accepted wisdom that the interests of businesses and regulators are fundamentally opposed, the bootleggers and Baptists model provides the insight that both groups stand to gain by cooperating to pass regulations, although their motivations may be different. As in the days of Sunday alcohol prohibition when both profit-seeking bootleggers and moralizing Baptists became strange bedfellows in their pursuit of a common policy, so too do environmental activists and big businesses frequently find themselves on the same side of a regulatory battle. Environmental regulations can help businesses by protecting them from competition.[13] Larger businesses, the profit-seeking "bootleggers," can easily absorb the high costs of regulation, but smaller firms cannot cope with these costs and cannot enter the market or are forced to leave it.[14] Environmental activists and regulators, the moralizing "Baptists," want regulations to be passed to improve the environment and expand their spheres of influence. In this way, the "Baptists" provide moral cover for many environmental regulations that benefit special interests, and this cover disguises cronyism as furthering the public interest.

Instances of cronyism stemming from environmental regulations abound. A regulation that mandated industrial scrubber requirements benefited the high-sulfur eastern US coal industry at the expense of the cleaner-burning western coal industry.[15] Regulators designed the Clean Air Act of 1970 to benefit established firms at the expense of newcomers by compelling only new firms to install expensive scrubbers at coal-fired electric plants and exempting established firms from this obligation.[16] A 1973 Supreme Court decision further tilted the playing field in favor of established firms by making the construction of new smelting plants more difficult for new competitors.

Economists Michael Maloney and Robert McCormick empirically tested the effect of the strengthened Clean Air Act and found that the tougher regulations benefited existing firms that saw their stock prices increase immediately following the ruling.[17] The same study analyzed the effects of a Department of Labor regulation on cotton-dust levels in textile factories and found that the stock prices of firms within the textile industry increased as the level of regulation increased. The Comprehensive Environmental Response, Compensation, and Liability Act of 1980, commonly known as "Superfund," was a boon to the waste management industry.[18] As Congress was drafting the law, industrial waste companies' stock values rose in tandem with the stringency of the environmental regulations.[19] In all these instances, lawmakers tailored regulations to benefit a specific firm or industry under the guise of protecting the environment. Despite the good intentions of citizens who advocate for stronger environmental protection through government intervention, the actual experience with environmental regulation demonstrates that special interests benefit when government regulators have the power to dole out protection. Cronies with political clout are able to tilt the regulatory playing field to their advantage.

Businesses are not the only cronies. Environmentalists seek to establish parks and wilderness recreation areas for their use, at taxpayers' expense, and those who run environmental organizations use personal connections to pursue their organizations' goals. This behavior is not unique to environmental groups, of course; politics works this way in general, and it is not surprising that the same type of cronyism that leads to corporate subsidies and bailouts also characterizes the political activities of nonprofit organizations. Environmental lobbyists use government funds and government connections to attract more funding from both government and private sources.[20] One organization, the Nature Conservancy, had nine employees making in excess of $200,000 a year in 2009 and in that same year had assets of $5.6 billion.[21]

Many donors, who believe they are giving funds to the organization so land can be conserved under its ownership, are unaware that the Nature Conservancy often sells land it acquires to the government at a substantial profit. While nominally funded by private donors, indirectly the government subsidizes the Nature Conservancy by knowingly paying well over the Nature Conservancy's purchase price for property.

While the Nature Conservancy's major activity is purchasing land to conserve it, other environmental organizations, like the Sierra Club, are designed specifically to lobby the government for environmental causes—that is, to use their connections in government to further their ends. Environmental regulatory bodies in the United States constitute one of the largest centralized planning structures that still exist in the modern world. It is therefore especially worrying that the political economy of environmental regulation lends itself to cronyism.

This analysis is not intended to indict environmentalism or environmental groups, any more than an analysis of crony capitalism is an indictment of capitalism. Rather, it illustrates that when the government becomes involved in resource allocation, the political process produces cronyism. Any time people want to accomplish goals that can be aided—or hindered—by political intervention, the system itself pulls people to develop connections to those who make the decisions, because discretionary decisions favor those with political connections. Surely the environmental community did not intend to promote the crony capitalism that led to subsidies to politically connected firms—with the Solyndra case being the most visible—but that was the result of a process that gives the government the power to make decisions and allocate resources rather than leaving that process to voluntary exchange within the market. There are liberal ways to further environmental protection, ranging from individual purchases of environmentally friendly technology and products to conservation easements purchased by environmental groups. The cases examined here show that ceding control to the government invites cronyism and often works against the goals that those who most support government intervention would have liked to achieve.

Environmentalism has been characterized as a movement in direct opposition to economic growth,[22] but when looking at the actual policies implemented in the name of protecting the environment, it becomes obvious that many businesses benefit from environmental politics. Many environmental policies have either been co-opted by special interests, or designed with their representatives—both corporate and environmental interests—at the table. The experience with environmental policy illustrates that cronyism will result when government representatives are in a position to favor some groups at the expense of others, regardless of the motivations. The veil of environmentalism has provided cover for politically connected businesses to profit and prevent competition, even as those in the environmental movement are able to profit from their activism.

CHAPTER 11:
SOCIAL JUSTICE

FROM A LIBERAL standpoint, social justice means that the law treats everyone the same and that the law protects everyone's basic human rights. Laws do not discriminate among individuals, and everyone has an equal opportunity under the law. The term most often refers to inequities among different classes of people, typically groups defined by their gender or ethnicity. However, advocates of social justice often extend the concept beyond this procedural view of justice to look at outcomes and to judge people as members of groups rather than as individuals. Proponents of this view argue that there is injustice if some groups, on average, have outcomes worse than those of other groups.

When equality of outcome is the goal, and when people are judged as members of groups rather than as individuals, social justice advocates see a role for the government to intervene to engage in transfers from some groups to others. Sometimes the transfers are of resources, but often they are transfers of opportunity, such as creating preferences for some groups over others or creating quotas for groups that advocates view as oppressed. When public policy pursues this outcome-based and group-based view of social justice, cronyism has an opportunity to play a role. The rules will tend to favor the members of politically well-connected groups at the expense of others.

This discussion is certainly not meant to minimize the importance of social justice or the importance of equal treatment under the law. Discrimination and institutionalized injustice have been present in the United States throughout much of its history. Race-based slavery existed in the United States until 1865, but discriminatory Jim Crow laws remained for another century. Women did not receive the constitutional right to vote until 1920, and they often did not have the same rights of property ownership as men did. These are examples of institutionalized discrimination, enforced by laws that provided legal rights to some that were not available to all. In these cases, the law granted privileges based on impersonal characteristics such as race and gender. The liberal remedy for such discrimination is to do away with discriminatory laws so that the law treats everyone equally. What often happens, however, is that when oppressed groups gain sufficient political power to remedy these violations of social justice, they use their power not just to eliminate the discrimination but to enact new laws that give them unique legal privileges. One group of cronies replaces another.

When new policies knock down government-created legal barriers or extend individual rights to a previously disenfranchised group, social justice policies help create a more liberal society and effectively eradicate privilege by giving everyone the same rights. When policies grant extra privileges to some groups that are not available to other groups, however, cronyism will result because the system creates political incentives for people to work for additional privileges for their groups.

The development of feminism provides a good example of how efforts to achieve social justice can result in cronyism. Feminism as a viable social movement was conceived during a period of tumultuous growth and social change in the late nineteenth and early twentieth centuries. Although the technological, productive, and scientific capabilities of the United States as a young global superpower had dramatically altered the nation's infrastructure and wealth, social arrangements had changed very little since the country's founding. The ruling legal paradigm, the doctrine of coverture, held that a husband and wife were one person in the eyes of the law, and the "very being or legal existence of the woman is suspended during the marriage," as documented by Engilsh jurist Sir William Blackstone in his 1765 *Commentaries on the Laws of England*. This standard prohibited married women from singly entering into contracts, owning property, or initiating legal action in the courts without the approval of their husbands.[1] From a property-rights perspective, the doctrine of coverture is antithetical to the ideal of self-ownership and is best conceptualized as a principal-agent relationship in which the husband legally owned his wife and her revenue stream.[2] Additionally, the government denied women the right to vote and therefore categorized them as a lower class of citizen.

After decades of organizing, petitioning, and challenging legal precedents in the courtroom, the law afforded women in the United States the full political rights that it had previously restricted to men. This first wave of feminism culminated with newly recognized political rights for women in the twentieth century, including the right to vote, and strengthened civil rights in the nineteenth and twentieth centuries, including the rights to enter into contracts and own property. The economic benefits of extending property rights to women have been considerable, as many studies note,[3] but the reforms that the first wave of feminism wrought also brought the United States closer to a standard of liberalism because they expanded the protection of individual rights and voluntary contract to a previously disenfranchised group. The economic benefits came because capitalism is the economic manifestation of liberalism. Liberal principles enabled the advancement of social justice.

Slavery in the pre–Civil War South provides an even starker example of laws that treated individuals differently, in this case based on race. Even after the abolition of slavery, discrimination in the form of Jim Crow laws continued into the 1960s. These laws constituted an obvious form of privilege for white Southerners at the expense of a politically crippled African American population. Discriminatory policies significantly curtailed African Americans' opportunities for success, an expected result from an illiberal system.[4] These diminished opportunities were the result of the cronyism that treated individuals differently under the law.

A series of Supreme Court decisions in the mid-twentieth century gradually chipped away at the edges of white racial privilege until the landmark case *Brown v. Board of Education* was decided in 1954. The passage of the Civil Rights Act of 1964 and the Voting Rights Act of 1965, which effectively ended legislative and political segregation in the United States, solidified this movement. The dissolution of Jim Crow laws moved the US government closer to the side of liberalism; by recognizing African Americans as legal equals of white Americans, the government removed the political favoritism afforded to white Americans and members of all groups were able to interact and compete on a level legal playing field.

The early victories for advocates of feminism and minority rights can be contrasted with their modern policy proposals. While the first wave of feminism and the 1950s civil rights movement focused on securing political rights that would grant women and blacks the same legal privileges historically afforded to white males, later iterations of feminism and social justice focused on rectifying perceived injustices in civil society by giving women and minorities privileges under the law that were not available to everyone.[5] Proponents of this new conception of justice expected the government not only to eliminate its discriminatory policies and biased privilege-granting, but also to provide a new set of discriminatory laws that favored members of those groups that had previously been discriminated against. Whereas in the past, the law denied women and minorities certain rights that were available to others, in the post–civil rights era, it guaranteed them certain privileges not available to others. The government established quotas for previously oppressed groups in school admissions, in job classifications, and even in intercollegiate athletics.

This new approach marks a dramatic shift in the comprehension of oppression and in the understanding of social justice, partly because it advocates giving privileges to some that are not available to others, and partly because it advocates granting these privileges to groups rather than treating people as individuals. This new view of social justice looks at group outcomes such as women's earnings compared to men's, or blacks' earnings compared to whites'. These group outcomes are the result of millions of decentralized decisions made by scattered economic actors in response to the decisions of other actors, as Hayek emphasized.[6]

Many feminists point to the relative lack of women in executive positions as an instance of oppression that the government must counteract. However, unlike the straightforward case of the government preventing women from owning property, the small number of female executives could be caused by a variety of factors, including differences in career decisions and life plans, differences in productivity, and differences in human capital endowments. Indeed, while fewer women than men are on corporate boards, some women are on corporate boards, and while the average incomes of blacks are lower than those of whites as a group, many individual blacks earn more than many individual whites, and many individual blacks have incomes higher than the average income for whites. In a liberal society, individuals have rights, and the government protects individual rights. The new social justice view of society argues for granting rights to groups based on the criterion that group outcomes should be equal. Equality of outcome replaces equality of opportunity as a social goal, and outcomes are based on group membership rather than on the treatment of people as individuals.

Despite the murkiness of women's grounds for claiming oppression, the governments of France, Spain,

Norway, the Netherlands, and Belgium have leaped to address this issue by mandating quotas for female representation on corporate executive boards. In those European countries, policymakers have chosen to pass laws that grant privileges to one group—women—over others. From a liberal perspective, this granting of privileges to one group is discriminatory in the same way as the laws that once favored white males over other groups.

In Norway, for example, the government mandated a quota of 40 percent female executive representation, a bold increase from the previous natural level of 9 percent. One study analyzed the gender quota's effects and found that affected firms suffered a sharp drop in stock prices after the policy's announcement.[7] Setting aside the economic effects, if firms select and promote employees based on group membership rather than individual merit, it creates the opportunity for connections to play a greater role than qualifications. Modern feminists and social justice advocates frequently call for new government privileges for protected classes. In this way, modern feminism and social justice theory have replaced one form of cronyism with another.

One significant area of feminist contention is the wage differential between industries that are primarily staffed by men and those that are predominantly staffed by women. Noting that average wages for female-dominated careers like nursing and elementary education were lower than those for male-dominated careers like truck driving and vocational education, many feminists concluded that systematic discrimination is to blame for this inequality in outcomes. Thus, the doctrine of "comparable worth," the idea that wages for jobs that are primarily worked by men should pay the same as comparable but different jobs that are primarily worked by women, was born. Experimental research on job evaluations under comparable worth policies suggests that implementing comparable pay may be not be possible.[8] The study found that three job evaluation firms presented wildly different value estimates for the same list of twenty-seven jobs. This finding suggests that job evaluations will tend to be tinged by the biases of the person doing the evaluating, opening the door to cronyism. The policy's structure privileges several groups: female laborers enjoy privilege over their employers who have to subsidize their artificially high wages, skilled female (and some male) laborers enjoy privilege over unskilled female laborers who are pushed out of the market, and consumers must pay higher prices to finance the policy.[9] Comparable worth policies do not offset previous privileges but rather create a host of new privileges and disadvantages.

Racial quotas and preferences for hiring and admission—affirmative action—are also policies that replace one kind of government privilege with another. Before the civil rights–era reforms, US government policy often provided advantages to white Americans while job training program administrators and public social service providers overlooked or sometimes deliberately ignored African American citizens. In documenting the many ways that African Americans were slighted while privileges went to white Americans during the 1930s and 1940s, political scientist and historian Ira Katznelson describes pre–civil rights public policy as "affirmative action for whites."[10] Following the liberalizing changes wrought by the civil rights movement, legislators were eager to atone for their discriminatory sins. Unfortunately, policymakers attempted to solve the problem of historical racial disenfranchisement by shifting the disenfranchisement to other groups.

Modern affirmative action in the United States has innocuous roots in John F. Kennedy's 1961 Executive Order 10925, which required government employees not to factor considerations of "race, creed, color, or national origin" into hiring decisions. Had this policy continued without revision, affirmative action would fall under the heading of liberalism because it would remove any favoritism for applicants because of their membership in a particular group. The idea behind Kennedy's policy was that people should be judged as individuals, not as members of groups. Four years later, however, Lyndon Johnson reengineered affirmative action by requiring the federal government to "promote the full realization of equal employment opportunity through a positive, continuing program in each executive department and agency" through Executive Order 11246. With the stroke of a pen, President Johnson changed affirmative action from the negation of privilege to the promotion of its full realization. Additionally, the adoption of affirmative action was fundamentally at odds with Title VII of the Civil Rights Act of 1964, which prohibits employers from discriminating against employees on the basis of race, color, religion, and other protected statuses. Subsequent legislative modifications and court decisions, notably Justice William Brennan's 1979 opinion issued in *United Steelworkers v. Weber*, swept this legal inconsistency under the rug. Justice Brennan's opinion affirmed employers' right to consider race in hiring decisions when it is done to "break down old patterns of segregation and hierarchy." In this way, the US government replaced the old state-sanctioned privileged class with a new state-sanctioned privileged class, this one with the potent moral authority of victimhood validating its existence. Affirmative action therefore is a form of cronyism in the same way that early policies that primarily benefited white Americans were a form of cronyism: affirmative action employs government force to tilt the scales of employment decisions in favor of one group at the expense of another. Judging people as members of groups rather than as individuals lays the foundation for cronyism. When some groups can be favored over others, people enter the political process to establish relationships that create privileges for their groups.

Affirmative action in university admissions has changed the application process from a meritocratic one to a system that also judges applicants based on arbitrary factors of race or class in order to engineer a state-approved level of diversity among the student body. In addition to the ethical issues involved in granting government privilege to one group over another, affirmative action has resulted in many negative unintended consequences for both its intended beneficiaries and for members of those groups who do not enjoy government privilege. A survey of college freshmen found that over half of the students surveyed opposed affirmative action policies and that the students who affirmative action policies most often discriminate against—whites and Asian Americans—were the most opposed.[11] Additionally, many scholars have questioned the proposition that affirmative action benefits minority students. Economist Thomas Sowell, for instance, points out that many African American students are admitted to more prestigious universities than their white counterparts with identical credentials are.[12] This policy has led to high drop-out rates among those African American students who are not academically prepared for the level of coursework for which schools artificially selected them. It also attaches a stigma to all minority students regardless of their qualifications, because people tend to think that schools admitted them because of affirmative action.

Focusing on increasing terminal outcomes, like the percentage of minorities employed in a certain industry, ignores the social and economic factors that make it difficult for minorities to achieve representative employment on their own.[13] While increased campus diversity is a desirable goal, the methods that affirmative action employs result in student resentment, minority under-preparedness, and discrimination against nonprotected students. The policy of affirmative action in university admissions has substituted yesterday's "good old boys" cronyism for an updated, politically correct form of cronyism.

The motivating forces behind feminism and social justice—the reaction against unjust government privilege of males and whites—were fruitful and necessary catalysts that established a more liberal society. The eradication of Jim Crow laws and the extension of economic rights to women were important steps toward eliminating the cronyism of the past. Modern advocates for social justice, however, have called for replacing the privileges that their activist predecessors fought so hard to destroy with a new set of privileges for a new set of privileged groups. Rather than advocating for social justice as an environment in which the law treats everyone as equal and everyone as an individual, social justice advocates push for one set of cronies to be replaced by another. Independent of any inherent unfairness, this system rewards people who use the political process to gain privileges for those who possess legally favored characteristics. When the law allows unequal treatment because of group characteristics, it encourages cronyism.

The ideologies of social justice have the potential to contribute to either liberalism or cronyism. In the cases where feminism and theories of social justice helped to eradicate privileges or extend them universally, these policies strengthened liberalism in the United States and reaffirmed the role of voluntary association in resource distribution. On the other hand, these same ideologies have in recent times tilted toward cronyism; policies like comparative worth and affirmative action legislatively grant privileges to certain groups at the expense of others, pushing those groups to use the political process to maintain and expand the favorable treatment the law provides to them.

Social justice is a sensitive topic—one that deserves a lengthy discussion partly because fairness is a justly important political goal and partly because in contemporary politics lawmakers and policy analysts often cite the goal of social justice as a reason for establishing laws that lead to cronyism. Creating an environment in which everyone has an equal opportunity is a noble goal, but if legislators pursue that goal by passing laws that favor some groups over others, they create political incentives for people to work to have their groups be favored. One result is that people substitute unproductive political activity for productive economic activity. Another result is that people in one group are distrustful, and sometimes resentful, toward people in other groups because of the differential privileges the institutional environment produces. The liberal approach to social justice is to treat everyone as an individual and to treat everyone as equal under the law. Differential privileges based on group membership lead away from liberalism and toward cronyism.

CHAPTER 12:
CRONY CAPITALISM
AND DEMOCRACY

A FTER THE BERLIN Wall collapsed in 1989 and the Soviet Union dissolved in 1991, Francis Fukuyama declared the establishment of democratic government and market economies as "the end of history," meaning that democracy and market-oriented economies were the final evolution of economic and political institutions.[1] Fukuyama's characterization of democratic government as the end of history understates the importance of constitutional constraints on government. "Democracies" do not operate under the principle that the government does whatever the majority wants; rather, democratic governments have constitutional constraints on the activities they can undertake.

The US Constitution provides a good example of a formal constitution that gives enumerated powers to the government—in other words, the government has only those powers that the Constitution specifically allows it. The constitutional framework of other Western democracies is similar, although every nation is different. Britain, for example, does not have a formal written constitution, but the constitutional rules that run British government are similar to those of the United States. The point is that the Western democracies that Fukuyama sees as the end of history do not make their political decisions democratically, if "democratically" means that governments carry out the majority's will. Rather, there are constitutional constraints and a fiscal constitution that limit the powers of those governments.

Over time, those constitutional constraints on the government have eroded so that the government has increasingly made its decisions with fewer constitutional constraints. Interest group politics has gained increasing influence over government decision-making, opening the door to crony capitalism and leading to what Olson has described as the decline of nations.[2] Democracy poses a danger to the economy because it opens the door to political pressures that lead to cronyism. The more that government decisions can be influenced by political pressures—that is, the more democratic a government is—the more a nation's economy will turn toward cronyism. For democracies to be productive rather than destructive, those who hold political power must work within clear constitutional constraints that limit their discretion—that is, that limit their ability to engage in cronyism. Western democracies have prospered not because of their democratic governments, but because of the constitutional constraints that have limited the powers of those governments.

Crony capitalism is the movement of capitalism away from liberalism and toward cronyism. Capitalism is based on private property rights, rule of law, and voluntary exchange. As the government gains more regulatory power to dictate the terms of exchange and more authority to alter the terms of exchange through taxes and subsidies, political connections displace economic productivity as the way to profitability. Government management of an economy means political connections matter, which means that cronyism will displace liberalism.

In 2011, the Occupy movement developed as a backlash against crony capitalism. Its first big protest went under the Occupy Wall Street banner, and one of the complaints people in the movement voiced was that after the housing bubble burst in 2008, the federal government moved to bail out big banks and other financial firms—AIG was notable for its $162 billion bailout[3]—while many homeowners lost their homes to foreclosure. Many of those in the Occupy movement called for greater government regulation and oversight of financial and other firms to control crony capitalism. But, as our analysis has shown in case after case, more government is not the cure for cronyism; it is the cause.

Economist John Taylor, analyzing the bailouts of banks and auto companies in 2008 and 2009, notes,

> Both the principles of economic freedom and the empirical evidence of what actually has gone wrong in the economy suggest quite clearly that the government did not need more power or more discretion to regulate more markets or more firms in the wake of the crisis. It already had plenty of power before then. Indeed, it was this very power and discretion that led inexorably to the favoritism, to the bending of the rules, to the reckless risk-taking, and, yes, to the bailouts. . . . This is textbook crony capitalism: the power of government and the rule of

men—rather than the power of the market and
the rule of law—to decide who will benefit and
who will not.[4]

Taylor goes on to document how cronyism led to excessive
risk-taking, partly through Fannie Mae and Freddie Mac,
partly as a result of the 2010 Dodd-Frank financial reform
act, and through the designation of politically connected
firms as "too big to fail."

When the government has the power to intervene in
people's economic affairs, to choose winners and losers,
and to designate some firms as worthy of government
bailouts while others must fend for themselves or go
under, people with political connections tend to benefit at
the expense of those lacking such connections. Additional
government oversight and control will push the economy
closer to the model of fascism, which we analyzed in
chapter 5. Critics of crony capitalism should be wary of
the argument that because of favoritism shown by those
in government to their cronies, the government should
have more power over the nation's economic affairs.

CHAPTER 13:
INDUSTRIAL POLICY

T HE TERM "INDUSTRIAL policy" describes the government's supporting of particular firms or industries to make them more competitive in the global economy. The post–World War II successes of the Japanese and South Korean economies have often been credited to an industrial policy that picks potential winners in the global marketplace and supports them through subsidies, favorable loan arrangements, tax benefits, and more direct benefits such as the use of eminent domain to provide them with land for their facilities. Industrial policy does not end in "ism," but it is no stretch to call industrial policy "favoritism" because it favors some firms or industries over others.

Post–World War II industrial policy began with Japan's desire to catch up with the developed world through state-planned industrial development in the aftermath of World War II. The economic planning boards created by the supreme commander for the Allied Powers (SCAP) during the US military occupation of Japan planted the seeds of Japan's industrial policy. The US occupation fundamentally changed the existing political institutions in Japan and rolled out radical labor, land, and antitrust reforms in addition to entrusting bureaucrats with expanded powers to intervene in economic affairs.[1] Political leaders in Japan were concerned that free trade and financial liberalization would prevent cartelized industries from growing and competing in the global market. In 1949, the government created the Ministry of International Trade and Industry (MITI). This agency had vast authority to regulate exports, raise tariffs, and direct public investment. This political restructuring destroyed many of the institutional norms that had traditionally tempered the collusion between business and government in Japan and set the stage for the state-driven industrialization policies that would characterize Japanese economic policy in the following decades. Japan expanded MITI's power after becoming sovereign in 1952 and used it as an important instrument with which to conduct the nation's ambitious industrialization policies.

Today, top government officials plucked from the most prestigious universities in the country still conduct industrial policy planning in Japan and discuss it with the most powerful businessmen in their respective industries. The lax enforcement mechanisms available to economic planning agencies prompt government officials to maintain informal ties with business leaders.[2] Officials utilize the "soft" powers of their offices to form relationships with the leaders of the critical industries in the national plan. Special interest groups in Japan tend to form in response to government industrialization initiatives rather than forming out of a desire to lobby for a policy in the first place.[3] State-driven industrialization in Japan has thus led to the development of rent-seeking "cottage industries" that cluster in whichever industry the government is attempting to stimulate. For this reason, the government was in a position to underrate promising innovations that businesses pitched to it.

Throughout its existence, MITI came dangerously close to preventing several innovative developments.[4] For instance, in the early 1950s, MITI initially prevented the development of an experimental transistor radio before relenting two years later and allowing the investment. Had MITI stuck with its original intuition, the company that created this early radio, Sony, might never have been given the chance to develop. Unfortunately, it is impossible to know what other promising innovations did not get the benefit of a second chance from the experts at MITI. We can see the firms and industries that thrived under MITI; we cannot see those that the government prevented from developing by favoring some over others.

Widespread corruption in Japanese industrial policy has led to inefficient investment and low growth.[5] Officials collude with businessmen to rig the competitive bidding process for public investment. In the practice of *dango*, the industry rotates which firm will win the bid and allows the chosen firm to secure a higher-than-normal contract amount. After they retire, the bureaucrats who engage in this corruption receive kickbacks and cushy positions in the firms that they regulated, a practice known as *amakudari*, or "the descent from heaven." Cronies receive benefits unavailable to outsiders. The growth of these corrupt practices has increased with the pace of the growth of government intervention in the Japanese economy. Sociologists Chikako Usui and Richard Colignon, for instance, find a positive relationship between the prevalence of amakudari within the country's financial sector and the growth of the Ministry of Finance (MOF) that regulates that sector.[6] Evidence of corruption between industry and government in state industrial planning calls into question the true motivation behind the plans.

Olson uses Japan as a prime example of the rise and decline of nations due to interest-group politics. He notes that after policy disruptions eliminate old political connections and networks, businesses concentrate on productive activity because they can no longer secure political favors.[7] Industrial policy in Japan favors some Japanese businesses over others, creating incentives for business leaders to develop political connections so that they can be among the privileged. Over time, connections become increasingly important to business profitability, and an entrepreneurial economy evolves into one in which success is based on political favoritism and cronyism. As we have noted in previous chapters, Olson argues that such a system leads to the decline of nations. Note that Olson made this argument in the early 1980s, well before Japan's financial crisis in 1991 that led to its "lost decade" of economic stagnation in the 1990s.

Japan's rapid economic growth in the 1950s and 1960s laid the foundation for South Korea to implement similar policies to try to join the global economic community with export-led growth.[8] Political power changed hands several times in the decades following the war's end before it was finally seized by Park Chung-hee, an ambitious military general with grand plans for the South Korean economy, in 1961. Park's leadership experience was steeped in military logistics and the planning of complex systems. He applied this regimented military knowledge to his new economic policy of "export-oriented industrialization." Inspired by the rapid military industrialization of the Japanese colony of Manchukuo, which he had witnessed as an officer in the Manchukuo imperial army, Park envisioned a period of rapid industrialization in South Korea aided by the expert guidance and resource assistance of planners in the central government. He and his advisers believed that unfettered competition and open financial markets would destroy South Korean businesses' opportunities to grow into powerful cartels that could compete against established Western companies in the global economy.

One of Park's first accomplishments was nationalizing the banking sector so that the state would be the sole source of investment funds in the country. Next, he turned to the task of securing the business alliances that he needed to make his vision a reality. To do this, his administration engaged in some friendly extortion. Park's subordinates rounded up the wealthiest businessmen in South Korea and threatened them with fines and jail time if they would not comply with the state's industrialization plans.[9] Many savvy businessmen accepted this plea bargain and cemented their status as protected members of society. With the business community in his pocket and the engine of financial investment in the service of the state, Park then rallied South Koreans around his policies with mantras that promised "nation-building through export" and "helping those [industries and firms] who help themselves." The South Korean government then proceeded to "help the industries and firms that helped themselves" by helping the politicians who protected them to succeed in the political arena.

Park's adoption of export-oriented industrialization in South Korea effectively changed the South Korean government into the board of directors for "Korea Inc." The government gave wealthy businessmen, academics, and government officials a voice in the biggest planning agencies in South Korea. These interest groups coordinated their efforts to build up the country's industrial capabilities and to catapult it into the ranks of the modern, developed economies.

A 1973 shift to investment in heavy industry and chemicals only cemented the economic might of family-owned South Korean cartels, called *chaebols*, at the expense of the working Koreans who paid higher prices for domestic goods. Agencies such as the Economic Planning Board and the Ministry of Trade and Industry used their arsenal of targeted subsidies, import restrictions, loan guarantees, and licensing requirements to strengthen the most promising South Korean businesses and "infant industries." The exchange of favors flowed freely between businesses and the politicians that helped them; corruption, bribery, favoritism, and clientelism dominated South Korean industrial policy.[10] There existed a dense web of personal contacts that exchanged private money for political favors: chaebols rewarded government agents with handsome donations in exchange for public loans and sweetheart deals. Government agents in South Korea sometimes cut out the middleman and directed the benefits straight to themselves: the Park administration kept around 10 percent of all public loans for personal and political uses.[11]

South Korean industrial policy gave rise to a backlash that caused working-class Koreans to demand "economic democracy," or the extension of government privileges primarily to the working class as a counterweight to decades of business privileges.[12] The economic democracy argument is that the government has favored one group of cronies for decades, preventing the working class from sharing in the benefits of industrialization. The supporters of economic democracy want to change the group of cronies who benefit from government favoritism from those who run big businesses to the workers. Such a change is plausible in a democracy, where workers control a substantial share of the votes. Regardless of the recipient, government-sanctioned favoritism tilts the playing field in a certain direction at the expense of competitors and taxpayers. If South Korea continues on its path toward expanded government privilege, the tide of cronyism in economic policy is not likely to reverse.

There is mixed evidence about the effectiveness of South Korean and Japanese industrial policy. Economists Raghuram Rajan and Luigi Zingales suggest that South Korea's and Japan's positions as developing nations with low contractibility and low capital opportunities in the wake of World War II made a relationship-based finance system more attractive in the beginning, but may be stifling growth in the present.[13] Both economies did grow considerably under these policies, but so did the economies of countries such as Hong Kong and Singapore that did not entrust the government to pick the winners and losers.[14] Others, such as economist Ben Powell, argue that the governments originally discouraged some of Japan's and South Korea's most successful businesses, while businesses that it supported have consistently not lived up to expectations.[15] The areas in which the Japanese government restricted competition to encourage growth, such as chemicals and software, are the industries that struggle the most.[16] The strongest sectors of the Japanese economy—automobiles, electronics, and robotics—are the areas in which the Japanese government restricted competition the least. Similarly, South Korea boasts the second-largest shipbuilding industry world, but its industrial policy has dulled the firms' competitiveness to the point where the industry depends on bailouts to survive. The connected chaebols in South Korea received larger shares of government assistance despite offering lower returns than smaller competing firms.[17] This evidence suggests that the South Korean and Japanese economies did not grow because of their industrial policies, but rather in spite of them.

The social costs of state-driven industrialization policies are significant. They deprive consumers of low prices and expanded choice while forcing them to subsidize the companies that lobbied for the policies. The benefits of East Asian industrial policy can charitably be called mixed; although Japan grew substantially from the 1950s through the 1980s, and South Korea's growth that started in the 1960s has continued into the twenty-first century, the industries that the government supported were not the only ones to drive this growth. Both countries started with the advantage of low wages and were able to adopt technologies that had been developed elsewhere. Their growth has slowed as they have approached the technological frontier and as wages rose so that they were no longer low-wage countries.

The degree to which Japan's and South Korea's industrial policies were responsible for their rapid growth is still up for debate; it is not clear that these industries would not have grown naturally without government protection as they did in other countries. What is clear is that the government granted privilege to a protected class at the expense of the common people. It turned the invisible hand of the market into the grabbing hand of cronyism, to use the terminology of economists Timothy Frye and Andrei Shleifer (although their examples come from post-communist countries rather than from the application of industrial policy).[18] The cronyism that developed in both Japan and Korea as a result of industrial policy is now undermining both countries' global competitiveness.

CHAPTER 14:
CRONYISM AND BIG
GOVERNMENT

T HE FEATURE THAT unites all forms of cronyism is that the power of government enables them. The bigger the government, measured both in its expenditures and its regulatory power, the bigger the potential for cronyism. The larger the government's budget, the more influence its tax and expenditure policies will have on business profitability and the prosperity of individuals. The larger the government's regulatory footprint, the more profitability and prosperity will be determined by regulatory favors rather than by productive activity. In this environment, people must become rent-seekers as a matter of economic survival. No matter how well-intentioned regulations are at their creation, over time regulatory agencies become "captured" by those they regulate so that regulations benefit the regulated rather than the general public.[1]

Big government not only steers businesses toward seeking political benefits, it often gives them no alternative but to engage in the political process to protect themselves from harm. The government often threatens to impose taxes or regulatory costs on businesses, pushing even those that want to avoid the political process to get involved in lobbying to protect themselves from predatory policies.[2] Businesses are then presented with two alternatives: either attempt to compete against cronies that have an unfair advantage, or become a crony to stay afloat. Those who don't engage in cronyism must bear the costs that cronies impose on them through government force.

One justification often given for expanding the scope of the government is that a bigger government presence in a market economy can help to control the abuses of cronyism. Once we understand the causes of cronyism, however, it becomes apparent that this reasoning is exactly backward. Government powers allow some interest groups to impose costs on others, which forces everyone to engage in the political process to compete to be the cronies who benefit from government interference. Big government does not control cronyism; it causes cronyism.

The common element that links all the economic and political systems discussed in this book, except for liberalism and capitalism (as liberalism's economic component), is that they all are based on the premise that people should turn over control of part of their lives and property to some form of collective organization—most commonly, the government—for the good of everybody. When this surrender happens, some people are able to control the resources of others for the benefit of some in the group and at a cost to others. While there may be a tendency for most people to favor those with whom they have relationships, in *The Road to Serfdom* Hayek explains (in a chapter titled "Why the Worst Get On Top") that the incentives inherent in government attract people into positions of power who want to use that power to their advantage.[3] We cannot evaluate economic and political systems under the assumption that those who hold power are omniscient, benevolent despots. Political and economic systems should be evaluated under the assumption that people who hold power will abuse it for their own benefit. Although not everyone is prone to commit such abuses, some people are, so political and economic institutions should be designed to guard against the possibility that the worst will get on top.[4]

People have designed many political and economic systems based on sophisticated analyses of social interactions that point to ways that society might be redesigned and improved. Fundamentally, however, all systems rest on either the principle that people control their own lives and property or the principle that some people should control the lives and property of others. The latter principle inevitably leads to a system in which the people who have connections to those with control benefit at the expense of those who do not. Despite sophisticated terminology and justifications, the choices reduce to liberalism versus cronyism.

CHAPTER 15:
LIBERALISM VERSUS
CRONYISM

T HROUGHOUT HISTORY, EVERYWHERE in the world, countries that have adopted capitalist economies have prospered, while those that have not have remained poor.[1] The capitalist institutions they describe are the institutions of liberalism: protection of property rights, rule of law, and freedom of exchange. Capitalism is the economic embodiment of the principles of liberalism. Alternatives to capitalism have been tried, ranging from government ownership of the means of production and central economic planning to government oversight of the market economy through industrial policy, fascism, corporatism, and other variants of managed capitalism. The common element that all these alternatives share is that they substitute group control—typically government control—of economic resources for private property and freedom of exchange. They do so to varying degrees, but in all cases government control means that the political process rather than voluntary exchange allocates resources, and that means that close connections to political power can steer resources toward cronies. The alternative to liberalism is cronyism.

Fukuyama's argument about capitalist democracies

being the end of history has its foundation in the general acceptance of the superiority of capitalism and democracy after the triumph of capitalist democracies in the Cold War. However, there is an inherent tension between capitalism and democracy that Fukuyama glosses over. Democratic government, like any government, has the ability to use force to transfer resources from some to others; that is, it has the ability to displace liberalism with cronyism. To think that when some can profit from political power people will not compete to obtain that power and to benefit from it is wishful thinking, and indeed dangerous thinking.

Despite the sophisticated labels attached to various political and economic systems, all come down to the alternative of allowing people to direct their energies and resources as they choose, or giving some people the power to direct the energies and resources of others. The first alternative is liberalism. The second is cronyism, but it is not always obvious that illiberal systems allocate power and resources through cronyism. We must take a few steps of reasoning to make this connection, because the systems themselves are designed to obscure the importance of personal connections. Regardless of the system's details, the first step is to recognize that if some people have the power to direct the resources and energies of others, people can use that power for their benefit. The next step is to see that for people to keep that power, they need the support of others. It then follows that they will use their power to benefit others in exchange for these others' support. The people with the power, and the people who support them, are the cronies. If those in power do not use their power to support cronies, competitors for that power will arise with another set of cronies to take that power away. Government regulation, taxation, and spending all lead to cronyism regardless of the specific system under which that government power is organized. Cronyism comes in many forms, but ultimately the only alternatives for political and economic systems are liberalism and cronyism.

No society finds itself at either extreme on the continuum between liberalism and cronyism, and the threat from people who will attempt to benefit from acquiring political power is always present. Ultimately, the only way to limit cronyism is to limit the government's power so that there is little benefit to participating in cronyism rather than productive activity. A common response to cronyism is to call for additional government regulation and oversight of markets, but bigger government often makes the problem worse. Politicians' using political power to their advantage causes cronyism, so a government with less regulatory power, and a government with a smaller budget, will be less prone to cronyism. A larger presence of government in an economy causes cronyism; it does not prevent it.

CHAPTER 16:
ECONOMIC AND
POLITICAL SYSTEMS

T HE WIDE VARIETY of economic and political systems analyzed here fall into either the category of individualism—where people make choices for themselves, their labor, and their property—or the category of collectivism, where some people have the power to make choices for everyone in the group. Collectivism may appear to imply that everyone in the collective has some say in group decisions, and the systems are designed to give that impression.[1] If people believe everyone has some say and that the government's programs are something citizens agreed to, it becomes easier for those with political power to obtain citizen compliance for their mandates.[2]

Democracy is the clearest case of such a system, because in a democracy government actions are the result of a democratic decision-making process that is open to all. But the reality is that some people have more decision-making power, and others have almost none. Democracy has the symbolic advantage that with one person, one vote, it appears that power is spread evenly. The reality is different, because those within the government have the power to force the policies they want onto others. Those with power support each other to maintain that power. Those are the cronies.

The people who have power support each other to maintain their power, whether the collective decision-making group is a democracy or a dictatorship, a socialist society or a capitalist one. Pure capitalism is the liberal economic system, but by interjecting government control through taxation, subsidies, regulation, and even the specter of government interference, a liberal economic system moves toward government control, which produces cronyism. Critics of crony capitalism tend to view themselves as critics of capitalism, but cronyism in crony capitalism exists because of growing government interference in the economy through taxation and regulation, not because of mutually beneficial market exchange.

Families tend to be run like communes, as collective organizations where members contribute for the good of the group, so it is instructive to consider why this arrangement works. Everyone in the family is a crony because each member relies on personal relationships with other family members for resources and support. When groups—even families—grow large enough that individuals have much closer personal relationships with some members of the group than with others, the collectivism of the group evolves into cronyism. Collectivism only works in groups that are small enough that everyone in the group can be in the same group of cronies. The model of the family, while it works well for a small group, does not scale up to function well with larger groups. Beyond small groups, liberalism allows individuals to deal with other individuals knowing that their arrangements will be for their mutual benefit. Voluntary exchange for the mutual benefit of those involved promotes cooperation, whereas the forcible transfer of resources from some to others pushes people to place themselves in the advantaged group that receives the transfers.

Ludwig von Mises notes that there are laws of social interaction that determine how political and economic systems will actually function. Commenting on social engineers who were unaware of such laws, Mises says,

> Philosophers had long since been eager to ascertain the ends which God or Nature was trying to realize in the course of human history.... But even those thinkers whose inquiry was free from any theological tendency failed utterly in these endeavors because they were committed to a faulty method. . . . They did not search for the laws of social cooperation because they thought that man could organize society as he pleased. If social conditions did not fulfill the wishes of reformers, if their utopias proved unrealizable, the fault was seen in the moral failure of man. Social problems were considered ethical problems. What was needed in order to construct the ideal society, they thought, was good princes and virtuous citizens. With righteous men any utopia might be realized.[3]

Our analysis illustrates Mises's point. Liberal political and economic systems build on the laws of social cooperation Mises references and are successful because they align the interests of all individuals so that everyone has an incentive to cooperate for the benefit of everyone else. Adam Smith explained this concept perhaps as eloquently as anyone when he noted that in a market economy, an invisible hand leads individuals pursuing their own interests to do what is best for everybody.[4] When individual interests are not aligned and the political or economic system forces some people to act in ways they would not without coercion, those who have the power to coerce can use that power for their benefit. Because no one individual has the power to coerce everyone else, those with power have the incentive to help each other, which is how cronyism develops. There are real differences among the political and economic systems this book has explored, but an examination of the decision-making processes within each of them reveals all these systems as variants of liberalism or cronyism.

In the real world, economic and political systems tend to fall somewhere in the middle of the spectrum, with elements of both liberalism and cronyism. In world history since the beginning of the Industrial Revolution, political and economic systems based on a large element of liberalism have prospered,[5] while those based on nonliberal systems have not. The danger, Olson pointed out, is that as political systems mature, they tend to move toward cronyism, which, to use Olson's language, leads to the decline of nations.[6] Understanding how that process works is the first step toward preventing it.

One motivation for undertaking this study was the recent backlash against crony capitalism. Critics noted that the government bailed out banks and other financial companies that held bad mortgages while homeowners lost their foreclosed homes. Energy companies with political connections received huge government subsidies, only to go bankrupt. Substantial funding from the Troubled Asset Relief Program (itself a manifestation of cronyism), approved to buy mortgage-backed securities, went to bail out bankrupt auto manufacturers, with sweetheart deals going to politically connected unions. The most common policy response to cronyism is to argue that more government oversight and more government regulation can curb cronyism, but decades of economic analysis show that government intervention is the cause of crony capitalism, not the cure.[7]

This book has expanded the analysis to look at political and economic systems beyond capitalism to illustrate that liberalism is the only way to curb cronyism. Can greater democratic oversight of the economic system curb cronyism? Perhaps an industrial policy to oversee the economy, as has been used in Japan and South Korea, can curb cronyism. By looking at how these systems and others have worked in practice, it becomes apparent that all alternatives to a liberal political and economic system lead to cronyism. History shows that socialism, fascism, and corporatism did not work well, and our analysis shows that despite the differences in their structures, because they were not liberal systems, politicians within each of them made decisions based on cronyism.

These historical analyses are valuable because they show how political and economic systems actually worked rather than conjecturing how they might work if the world were populated by "good princes and virtuous citizens," to use Mises's phrase.[8] But the dangers of cronyism also lie in the contemporary push to provide "rights" to natural amenities like animals and sand dunes, as the environmental movement often advocates, or even in movements designed to further social justice by remedying past injustices. While recognizing that injustices have occurred in the past—supported by government policies that limited individual rights or actually enslaved people—the appropriate remedy is the establishment of a liberal society based on voluntary agreement and mutually beneficial exchange. Too often, when a group gets sufficient political power to overturn past injustices, it uses that power to promote one group of cronies over another.

Except for liberalism, and capitalism as the economic component of liberalism, these various political and economic systems are all, in their essence, systems where some people can use their political and economic power to benefit their cronies at the general public's expense. This statement is true whether the entity in power is a political majority or a lone dictator. As Mises noted, the utopias promised by these political and economic systems proved unrealizable because they were committed to a faulty method.[9] When the government organizes a society so that individuals must give up some of their rights to the group's control, that society devolves into cronyism. Our analysis shows that this outcome has occurred in one case after another. Ultimately, the choice of political and economic systems comes down to the choice between liberalism and cronyism.

NOTES

INTRODUCTION

1. Friedrich A. Hayek, *The Road to Serfdom* (Chicago: University of Chicago Press, 1944); Milton Friedman, *Capitalism and Freedom* (Chicago: University of Chicago Press, 1962).

2. Joseph A. Schumpeter, *Capitalism, Socialism, and Democracy* (London: George Allen and Unwin, 1943).

3. Francis Fukuyama, *The End of History and the Last Man* (New York: Free Press, 1992).

4. Murray J. Edelman, *The Symbolic Uses of Politics* (Urbana: University of Illinois Press, 1985).

5. This book analyzes political and economic systems, or political economy. Religious and spiritual systems fall outside our analysis. However, examples as diverse as the rise of radical Islam in the twenty-first century and the influence of the Roman Catholic Church in the Middle Ages show that religion has an obvious influence on politics. Furthermore, Christian fundamentalism has an impact on politics in the contemporary United States. Our analysis could easily be extended to religious belief systems since people hold similar types of beliefs about religious systems as they do about political and economic systems. Robert Nelson even depicts environmentalism (and economics!) as a religion; see Robert H. Nelson, *The New Holy Wars: Economic Religion vs. Environmental Religion in Contemporary America* (University Park, PA: Pennsylvania State University Press, 2010). We consider environmentalism in chapter 10.

CHAPTER 1: LAYING A FOUNDATION

1. Even "public charity" is not accurate. It is government, not public, and it is a coerced transfer, not charity. An accurate descriptive term would be "coerced transfers through government." Still, the change in terminology to avoid the stigma had only a temporary effect, and today "welfare" has the same negative connotation as "public charity."

2. John Locke, *Two Treatises of Government* (Cambridge: Cambridge University Press, [1690] 1967).

3. Bernard Bailyn, *The Ideological Origins of the American Revolution*, enlarged ed. (Cambridge, MA: Belknap Press, 1992).

4. Thomas Hobbes, *Leviathan* (New York: E. P. Dutton, [1651] 1950).

5. David A. Stockman, *The Great Deformation: The Corruption of Capitalism* (New York: PublicAffairs, 2013).

6. Ludwig von Mises, *Human Action*, Scholar's Edition (Auburn, AL: Ludwig von Mises Institute, 1998), 2.

7. For good examples that lay the foundation for this approach to public policy analysis, see Francis Bator, "The Simple Analytics of Welfare Maximization," *American Economic Review* 67 (1957): 22–59; and J. de V. Graaf, *Theoretical Welfare Economics* (Cambridge: Cambridge University Press, 1957).

8. Kenneth J. Arrow and Gerard Debreu, "Existence of an Equilibrium for a Competitive Economy," *Econometrica* 22, no. 3 (July 1954): 256–91.

9. Francis Bator, "The Anatomy of Market Failure," *Quarterly Journal of Economics* 72, no. 3 (August 1958): 351–79.

10. Hayek shows why the government does not have sufficient information to solve such problems in "The Use of Knowledge in Society." Buchanan shows the political problems involved, and Kohn and Holcombe offer critical analyses of this method. See Friedrich A. Hayek, "The Use of Knowledge in Society," *American Economic Review* 35, no. 4 (September 1945): 519–30; James M. Buchanan, "Public Finance and Public Choice," *National Tax Journal* 28 (December 1975): 383–94; Meir Kohn, "Value and Exchange," *Cato Journal* 24, no. 4 (Fall 2004): 303–39; and Randall G. Holcombe, "Make Economics Policy-Relevant: Depose the Omniscient Benevolent Dictator," *Independent Review* 17, no. 2 (Fall 2012): 1–12.

11. Hayek, "Use of Knowledge in Society."

12. William A. Niskanen, *Bureaucracy and Representative Government* (Chicago: Aldine-Atherton, 1971).

13. Barry R. Weingast, Kenneth A. Shepsle, and Christopher Johnsen, "The Political Economy of Benefits and Costs: A Neoclassical Approach to Distributive Politics," *Journal of Political Economy* 89, no. 4 (August 1981): 642–64.

14. Bruce Bueno de Mesquita et al., *The Logic of Political Survival* (Cambridge, MA: MIT Press, 2003); William A. Niskanen, *Autocratic, Democratic, and Optimal Government: Fiscal Choices and Economic Outcomes* (Cheltenham, UK: Edward Elgar, 2003).

CHAPTER 2: CAPITALISM

1. Locke, *Two Treatises of Government*.

2. Karl Marx and Friedrich Engels listed government production of education as a key aspect of the socialism they advocated in *The Communist Manifesto*.

3. David Friedman, *The Machinery of Freedom* (La Salle, IL: Open Court Press, 1973); Murray N. Rothbard, *For a New Liberty* (New York: Collier Books, 1973).

4. Murray N. Rothbard, *The Ethics of Liberty* (Atlantic Highlands, NJ: Humanities Press, 1982).

5. Friedrich A. Hayek, *The Constitution of Liberty* (Chicago: University of Chicago Press, 1960); Ayn Rand, *The Virtue of Selfishness* (New York: New American Library, 1957).

6. Joel Mokyr, *The Lever of Riches* (Oxford: Oxford University Press, 1990); David S. Landes, *The Wealth and Poverty of Nations: Why Some Are So Rich and Some So Poor* (New York: W. W. Norton, 1998).

7. James Gwartney and Robert Lawson, *Economic Freedom of the World 2012 Annual Report* (Vancouver: Fraser Institute, 2012).

CHAPTER 3: SOCIALISM

1. Gerald Segal, "China and the Disintegration of the Soviet Union," *Asian Survey* 32, no. 9 (1992): 848–68.

2. Ibid.

3. Richard R. Fagen, "Cuba and the Soviet Union," *Wilson Quarterly* 2, no. 1 (1978): 69–78.

4. Peter J. Boettke and Gary M. Anderson, "Soviet Venality: A Rent-Seeking Model of the Communist State," *Public Choice* 93 (1997): 37–53.

5. Paul Gregory and Mark Harrison, "Allocation under Dictatorship: Research in Archives," *Journal of Economic Literature* 43, no. 3 (2005): 721–61.

6. R. W. Davies, "Making Economic Policy," in Paul Gregory, ed., *Behind the Façade of Stalin's Command Economy* (Palo Alto, CA: Hoover Institution Press, 2001).

7. Mark Harrison, "The Political Economy of a Soviet Military R&D Failure: Steam Power for Aviation, 1932 to 1939," *Journal of Economic History* 63, no. 1 (2003): 178–212.

8. Andrei Markevich and Paul Gregory, "Creating Soviet Industry: The House That Stalin Built," *Slavic Review* 61, no. 4 (2002): 787–814.

9. Hayek, *Road to Serfdom*.

10. Archibald R. M. Ritter, "Entrepreneurship, Microenterprise, and Public Policy in Cuba: Promotion, Containment, or Asphyxiation?," *Journal of Interamerican Studies and World Affairs* 40, no. 2 (1998): 63–94.

11. Jean C. Oi, "Communism and Clientelism: Rural Politics in China," *World Politics* 37, no. 2 (1985): 238–66.

12. James Heinzen, "The Art of the Bribe: Corruption and Everyday Practice in the Late Stalinist USSR," *Slavic Review* 66, no. 3 (2007): 389–412.

13. Robert A. Packenham, "Capitalist Dependency and Socialist Dependency: The Case of Cuba," *Journal of Interamerican Studies and World Affairs* 28, no. 1 (1986): 59–92.

14. Alena Ledeneva, "Blat and Guanxi: Informal Practices in Russia and China," *Comparative Studies in Society and History* 50, no. 1 (2008): 118–44.

15. Ritter, "Entrepreneurship, Microenterprise, and Public Policy in Cuba."

16. Oi, "Communism and Clientelism."

17. Marcus Noland and Stephan Haggard, "Economic Crime and Punishment in North Korea" (Pearson Institute for Economics Working Paper No. 10-2, 2010).

18. John M. Kramer, "Political Corruption in the U.S.S.R.," *Western Political Quarterly* 30, no. 2 (1977): 213–24.

19. Paul Gregory and Valery Lazarev, "The Wheels of a Command Economy: Allocating Soviet Vehicles," *Economic History Review, New Series* 55, no. 2 (2002): 324–48.

20. Abram Bergson, "Income Inequality under Soviet Socialism," *Journal of Economic Literature* 22, no. 3 (1984): 1052–99.

21. Carmelo Mesa-Lago, "Growing Economic and Social Disparities in Cuba: Impact and Recommendations for Change," Report for the Cuba Transition Project of the Institute for Cuban and Cuban-American Studies at the University of Miami, 2002.

22. Martin King Whyte, "Inequality and Stratification in China," *China Quarterly* 64 (1975): 684–711.

23. Oleg Khlevnyuk and R. W. Davies, "The End of Rationing in the Soviet Union, 1934–1935," *Europe-Asia Studies* 51, no. 4 (1999): 557–609.

24. *Pravda*, November 13, 1973, quoted in Kramer, "Political Corruption in the U.S.S.R."

25. Andrei Shleifer and Robert Vishny, "Corruption," *Quarterly Journal of Economics* 108, no. 3 (August 1993): 599–617.

26. Markevich and Gregory, "Creating Soviety Industry."

CHAPTER 4: COMMUNISM

1. Karl Marx, "Critique of the Gotha Program, Part I," http://www.marxists.org/archive/marx/works.1875/gotha/ch01.htm.

2. Byung-Joon Ahn, "The Political Economy of the People's Commune in China: Changes and Continuities," *Journal of Asian Studies* 34, no. 3 (1975): 631–58.

3. Jean C. Oi, "Peasant Households between Plan and Market: Cadre Control over Agricultural Inputs," *Modern China* 12, no. 2 (1986): 230–51.

4. Jürgen Domes, "New Policies in the Communes: Notes on Rural Societal Structures in China, 1976–1981," *Journal of Asian Studies* 41, no. 2 (1982): 253–67.

5. Ibid.

6. Alan P. L. Liu, "The Politics of Corruption in the People's Republic of China," *American Political Science Review* 77, no. 3 (1983): 602–23.

7. Victor Nee, "Social Inequalities in Reforming State Socialism: Between Redistribution and Markets in China," *American Sociological Review* 56, no. 3 (1991): 267–82.

8. Andrew G. Walder, "Markets and Income Inequality in Rural China: Political Advantage in an Expanding Economy," *American Sociological Review* 67, no. 2 (2002): 231–53.

9. Jonathan Haidt, "Beyond Beliefs: Religions Bind Individuals into Moral Communities," *Personality and Social Psychology Review* 14, no. 1 (2010): 140–50.

10. Reuven Shapira, "Can We Comprehend Radical Social Movements without Deciphering Leadership Changes? Leaders' Survival and USSR Reverence in Kibbutzim," paper presented at the Israeli Anthropological Association Annual Conference, May 2008.

11. David De Vries and Eldad Shalem, "Dependence on the State and the Crisis of the Kibbutz: The System of Concentrated Credit in the 1960s and 1970s," Journal of Rural Cooperation 27, no. 2 (1999): 87–106.

12. This can be explained by the framework put forth in Mancur Olson's theory of collective action. See Mancur Olson, *The Logic of Collective Action* (Cambridge, MA: Harvard University Press, 1971).

13. Ran Abramitzky, "The Effect of Redistribution on Migration: Evidence from the Israeli Kibbutz," *Journal of Public Economics* 93 (2009): 498–511.

14. Ivan Vallier, "Structural Differentiation, Production Imperatives and Communal Norms: The Kibbutz in Crisis," *Social Forces* 40, no. 3 (1962): 233–42.

15. Peter J. Boettke, *Why Perestroika Failed: The Politics and Economics of Socialist Transformation* (London: Routledge, 1993).

CHAPTER 5: FASCISM

1. Peter Temin, "Soviet and Nazi Economic Planning in the 1930s," *Economic History Review* 44, no. 4 (1991): 573–93.

2. Arthur Schweitzer, "Big Business and the Nazi Party in Germany," *Journal of Business of the University of Chicago* 19, no. 1 (January 1946): 1–24.

3. Raymond G. Stokes, "The Oil Industry in Nazi Germany, 1936–1945," *Business History Review* 59, no. 2 (1985): 254–77.

4. Henry Ashby Turner Jr., "Hitler's Secret Pamphlet for Industrialists, 1927," *Journal of Modern Haistory* 40, no. 3 (1968): 348–74.

5. Arthur Schweitzer, "Big Business and Private Property under the Nazis," *Journal of Business of the University of Chicago* 19, no. 2 (April 1946): 99–126.

6. Thomas Ferguson and Hans-Joachim Voth, "Betting on Hitler: The Value of Political Connections in Nazi Germany," *Quarterly Journal of Economics* 123, no. 1 (2008): 101–37.

7. Stokes, "Oil Industry in Nazi Germany."

8. Ibid.

9. Ibid.

10. Ibid.

11. Philip C. Newman, "Key German Cartels under the Nazi Regime," *Quarterly Journal of Economics* 62, no. 4 (1948): 576–95.

12. Schweitzer, "Big Business and Private Property under the Nazis."

13. Ibid.

14. Ibid.

15. Schweitzer, "Big Business and the Nazi Party."

16. Temin, "Soviet and Nazi Economic Planning."

CHAPTER 6: CORPORATISM

1. Howard J. Wiarda, *Corporatism and Comparative Politics: The Other Great "Ism"* (Armonk, NY: M. E. Sharpe, 1996).

2. Walter Connor, *Tattered Banners: Labor, Conflict, and Corporatism in Postcommunist Russia* (New York: Westview, 1996).

3. L. P. Carpenter, "Corporatism in Britain, 1930–45," *Journal of Contemporary History* 11, no. 1 (1976): 3–25.

4. Paul G. Buchanan, "State Corporatism in Argentina: Labor Administration under Peron and Ongania," *Latin American Research Review* 20, no. 1 (1985): 61–95.

5. Nuno Luís Madureira, "Cartelization and Corporatism: Bureaucratic Rule in Authoritarian Portugal, 1926–45," *Journal of Contemporary History* 42, no. 1 (2007): 79–96.

6. Mario Pomini, "The Great Depression and the Corporatist Shift of Italian Economists," *European Journal of the History of Economic Thought* 18, no. 5 (2011): 733–53.

7. Sheldon Richman, "Fascism," *The Concise Encyclopedia of Economics* (Library of Economics and Liberty, 2008).

8. Ibid.

9. Roland Sarti, "Fascist Modernization in Italy: Traditional or Revolutionary?," *American Historical Review* 75, no. 4 (1970): 1029–45.

10. Mariuccia Salvati, "The Long History of Corporatism in Italy: A Question of Culture or Economics?," *Contemporary European History* 15, no. 2 (2006): 223–44.

11. Paul Corner, "Everyday Fascism in the 1930s: Centre and Periphery in the Decline of Mussolini's Dictatorship," *Contemporary European History* 15, no. 2 (2006): 195–222.

12. Jonathan Morris, "Contesting Retail Space in Italy: Competition and Corporatism 1915–1960," *International Review of Retail, Distribution and Consumer Research* 9, no. 3 (1999): 291–306.

13. Pomini, "Great Depression."

CHAPTER 7: DESPOTISM

1. Milan W. Svolik, *The Politics of Authoritarian Rule* (New York: Cambridge University Press, 2012).

2. Bueno de Mesquita et al., *Logic of Political Survival*; Niskanen, *Autocratic, Democratic, and Optimal Government*.

3. Mark Irving Lichbach, *The Rebel's Dilemma* (Ann Arbor: University of Michigan Press, 1995); Peter Kurrild-Klitgaard, *Rational Action, Collective Action, and the Paradox of Rebellion* (Copenhagen: University of Copenhagen, 1996).

4. Daron Acemoglu and James Robinson, *Why Nations Fail: The Origins of Power, Prosperity, and Poverty* (New York: Crown Publishing Group, 2012).

5. George B. N. Ayittey, "The African Development Conundrum," chapter 6 in Benjamin Powell, ed., *Making Poor Nations Rich: Entrepreneurship and the Process of Economic Development* (Stanford, CA: Stanford Business and Finance, 2008), 168.

CHAPTER 8: PROGRESSIVISM

1. Terry L. Anderson and Peter J. Hill, *The Birth of a Transfer Society* (Stanford: Hoover Institution Press, 1980).

2. Robert Higgs, *Crisis and Leviathan: Critical Episodes in the Growth of American Government* (New York: Oxford University Press, 1987).

3. Randall G. Holcombe, *From Liberty to Democracy: The Transformation of American Government* (Ann Arbor: University of Michigan Press, 2002).

4. Mancur Olson Jr., *The Rise and Decline of Nations* (New Haven, CT: Yale University Press, 1982).

5. William J. Baumol, "Entrepreneurship: Productive, Unproductive, and Destructive," *Journal of Political Economy* 98, no. 5, part 1 (October 1990): 893–921; William J. Baumol, *Entrepreneurship, Management, and the Structure of Payoffs* (Cambridge, MA: MIT Press, 1993).

CHAPTER 9: MAJORITARIANISM

1. Holcombe, *From Liberty to Democracy.*

2. The Twelfth Amendment changed the top five vote-getters to the top three vote-getters. The Constitution specifies that the electors meet in their states to cast their votes. This requirement prevents the electors from colluding to choose a president and increases the odds that the House will make the final decision.

3. Weingast, Shepsle, and Johnsen, "Political Economy of Benefits and Costs."

4. Douglass C. North, John Joseph Wallis, and Barry R. Weingast, *Violence and Social Orders: A Conceptual Framework for Interpreting Recorded Human History* (Cambridge: Cambridge University Press, 2009); Acemoglu and Robinson, *Why Nations Fail.*

5. Acemoglu and Robinson, *Why Nations Fail.*

CHAPTER 10: ENVIRONMENTALISM

1. Terry L. Anderson and Donald R. Leal, *Free Market Environmentalism,* revised ed. (London: Palgrave Macmillan, 2001).

2. Nelson, *New Holy Wars.*

3. Ibid.

4. For one example of this argument, see John A. Herrick, "Federal Project Financing Incentives for Green Industries: Renewable Energy and Beyond," *Natural Resources Journal* 43, no. 77 (2003): 77–110.

5. Government Accountability Office, *DOE Loan Guarantees: Further Actions Are Needed to Improve Tracking and Review of Applications*, Report to Congressional Committees, GAO-12-157, March 2012.

6. Veronique de Rugy, "Assessing the Department of Energy Loan Guarantee Program," Testimony before the House Committee on Oversight and Government Reform, June 19, 2012, http:// oversight.house.gov/wp-content/uploads/2012/06/DeRugy -Testimony.pdf.

7. Ibid.

8. Diana Furchtgott-Roth, *Regulating to Disaster: How Green Jobs Policies Are Damaging America's Economy* (Jackson, TN: Encounter Books, 2012).

9. Peter Schweizer, *Throw Them All Out: How Politicians and Their Friends Get Rich off Insider Stock Tips, Land Deals, and Cronyism That Would Send the Rest of Us to Prison* (Boston: Houghton Mifflin Harcourt, 2011).

10. Carol Leonnig and Joe Stephens, "Federal Funds Flow to Clean-Energy Firms with Obama Administration Ties," *Washington Post*, February 14, 2012, http://articles.washingtonpost.com/2012-02 -14/politics/35444143_1_clean-tech-clean-energy-investment -program-venture-firms.

11. Darryl Siry, "In Role as Kingmaker, the Energy Department Stifles Innovation," *Wired*, December 1, 2009, http://www.wired.com /autopia/2009/12/doe-loans-stifle-innovation/.

12. Bruce Yandle, "Bootleggers and Baptists: The Education of a Regulatory Economist," *Regulation* 7, no. 3 (1983): 12–16.

13. George J. Stigler, "The Theory of Economic Regulation," *Bell Journal of Economics and Management Science* 2 (Spring 1971): 3–21.

14. An empirical study by Thomas Dean and Robert Brown supports the theory that environmental regulations deter firm entry and stifle competition. See Thomas Dean and Robert Brown, "Pollution Regulation as a Barrier to New Firm Entry: Initial Evidence and Implications for Future Research," *Academy of Management Journal* 38, no. 1 (1995): 288–303.

15. Bruce Ackerman and William Hassler, *Clean Coal/Dirty Air; or, How the Clean Air Act Became a Multibillion-Dollar Bail-Out for High-Sulfur Coal Producers* (New Haven, CT: Yale University Press, 1981).

16. Bruce Yandle, "Bootleggers and Baptists in Retrospect," *Regulation* 22, no. 3 (1999): 5–7.

17. Michael T. Maloney and Robert E. McCormick, "A Positive Theory of Environmental Quality Regulation," *Journal of Law and Economics* 25, no. 1 (1982): 99–123.

18. Todd Zywicki, "Environmental Externalities and Political Externalities: The Political Economy of Environmental Regulation and Reform," *Tulane Law Review* 73 (1999): 845–922.

19. Brett A. Dalton, David Riggs, and Bruce Yandle, "The Political Production of Superfund: Some Financial Market Results," *Eastern Economic Journal* 22, no. 1 (1996): 79–86.

20. Ron Arnold, *Undue Influence: Wealthy Foundations, Grant-Driven Environmental Groups, and Zealous Bureaucrats That Control Your Future* (Madison, WI: Free Enterprise Press, 1999).

21. The figures come from Ron Arnold's Green Tracking Library, "The Nature Conservancy," accessed December 19, 2012, http://undueinfluence.com/nature_conservancy.htm.

22. Nelson, *New Holy Wars*.

CHAPTER 11: SOCIAL JUSTICE

1. Reva B. Siegel, "The Modernization of Marital Status Law: Adjudicating Wives' Rights to Earnings, 1860–1930" (Yale Faculty Scholarship Series, Paper 1093, 1995).

2. Rick Geddes and Dean Lueck, "The Gains from Self-Ownership and the Expansion of Women's Rights," *American Economic Review* 92, no. 4 (2002): 1079–92.

3. B. Zorina Khan, "Married Women's Property Laws and Female Commercial Activity: Evidence from United States Patent Records, 1790–1895," *Journal of Economic History* 56, no. 2 (1996): 356–88; Geddes and Lueck, "Gains from Self-Ownership"; Carmen Diana Deere and Magdalena Leon, *Empowering Women: Land and Property Rights in Latin America* (Pittsburgh, PA: University of Pittsburgh Press, 2001).

4. Robert Higgs, "Accumulation of Property by Southern Blacks before World War I," *American Economic Review* 72, no. 4 (1982): 726–37.

5. Susan Williams, "A Feminist Reassessment of Civil Society," *Indiana Law Journal* 22, no. 2 (1997): 417–47; Jean L. Cohen and Andrew Arato, *Civil Society and Political Theory* (Cambridge, MA: MIT Press, 1994).

6. Hayek, *Constitution of Liberty*.

7. Kenneth R. Ahern and Amy K. Dittmar, "The Changing of the Boards: The Impact of Firm Valuation of Mandated Female Board Representation," *Quarterly Journal of Economics* 127, no. 1 (2012): 137–97.

8. E. Jane Arnault et al., "An Experimental Study of Job Evaluation and Comparable Worth," *Industrial and Labor Relations Review* 54, no. 4 (2001): 806–15.

9. June E. O'Neill, "Comparable Worth," *The Concise Encyclopedia of Economics* (Library of Economics and Liberty, 1993).

10. Ira Katznelson, *When Affirmative Action Was White: An Untold History of Racial Inequality in Twentieth-Century America* (New York: W. W. Norton & Company, 2006).

11. Linda J. Sax and Marisol Arredondo, "Student Attitudes in College Admissions," *Research in Higher Education* 40, no. 4 (1999): 439–59.

12. Thomas Sowell, "The Plight of Black Students in the United States," *Daedalus* 103, no. 2, Slavery Colonialism and Racism (1974): 179–94.

13. Richard Delgado, "Affirmative Action as a Majoritarian Device; or, Do You Really Want to Be a Role Model?," *Michigan Law Review* 89, no. 9 (1991): 1222–31.

CHAPTER 12: CRONY CAPITALISM AND DEMOCRACY

1. Fukuyama, *End of History*.

2. Olson, *Rise and Decline of Nations*.

3. That bailout consisted of Treasury funds of $70 billion, a $60 billion line of credit, and the purchase of $52.5 billion in mortgage-backed securities by the Federal Reserve Bank. See Hugh Son, "AIG's Trustees Shun 'Shadow Board,' Seek Directors (Update2)," *Bloomberg*, May 13, 2009, www.bloomberg.com/apps/news?pid=newsarchive&sid=aaog3i4yUopo.

4. John B. Taylor, *First Principles: Five Keys to Restoring America's Prosperity* (New York: W. W. Norton, 2012), 146.

CHAPTER 13: INDUSTRIAL POLICY

1. Shigeto Naka, Wayne T. Brough, and Kiyokazu Tanaka, "The Political Economy of Post-WWII Japanese Development: A Rent-Seeking Perspective," in Peter J. Boettke, ed., *The Collapse of Development* (New York: NYU Press, 1994), 256–88.

2. Victor D. Lippit, "Economic Planning in Japan," *Journal of Economic Issues* 9, no. 1 (1975): 39–58.

3. Eamonn Fingleton, "Japan's Invisible Leviathan," *Foreign Affairs* 74, no. 2 (1995): 69–85.

4. David R. Henderson, "Japan and the Myth of MITI," *The Concise Encyclopedia of Economics* (Library of Economics and Liberty, 1993).

5. William K. Black, "The 'Dango' Tango: Why Corruption Blocks Real Reform in Japan," *Business Ethics Quarterly* 14, no. 4 (2004): 603–23.

6. Chikako Usui and Richard A. Colignon, "Government Elites and Amakudari in Japan, 1963–1992," *Asian Survey* 35, no. 7 (1995): 682–98.

7. Olson, *Rise and Decline of Nations.*

8. Sudip Chaudhuri, "Government and Economic Development in South Korea, 1961–79," *Social Scientist* 24, no. 11/12 (1996): 18–35.

9. Young Back Choi, "Industrial Policy as the Engine of Economic Growth in South Korea: Myth and Reality," in Peter J. Boettke, ed., *The Collapse of Development* (New York: NYU Press, 1994), 231–55.

10. David C. Kang, "Bad Loans to Good Friends: Money Politics and the Developmental State in South Korea," *International Organization* 56, no. 1 (2002): 177–207.

11. Choi, "Industrial Policy."

12. Randall G. Holcombe, "South Korea's Economic Future: Industrial Policy, or Economic Democracy?," *Journal of Economic Behavior & Organization* 88 (April 2013): 3–13.

13. Raghuram Rajan and Luigi Zingales, "Which Capitalism? Lessons from the East Asian Crisis," *Journal of Applied Corporate Finance* 11, no. 3 (1998): 40–48.

14. Choi, "Industrial Policy."

15. Ben Powell, "State Development Planning: Did It Create an East Asian Miracle?" *Review of Austrian Economics* 18, no. 2/3 (2005): 305–23.

16. Michael E. Porter and Mariko Sakakibara, "Competition in Japan," *Journal of Economic Perspectives* 18, no. 1 (2004): 27–50.

17. Anne O. Krueger and Jungho Yoo, "Falling Profitability, Higher Borrowing Costs, and Chaebol Finances during the Korean Crisis," in David T. Coe and Se-Jik Kim, eds., *Korean Crisis and Recovery* (Washington, DC: International Monetary Fund, 2002), 161–96.

18. Timothy Frye and Andrei Shleifer, "The Invisible Hand and the Grabbing Hand," *American Economic Review* 87, no. 2 (May 1997): 354–58.